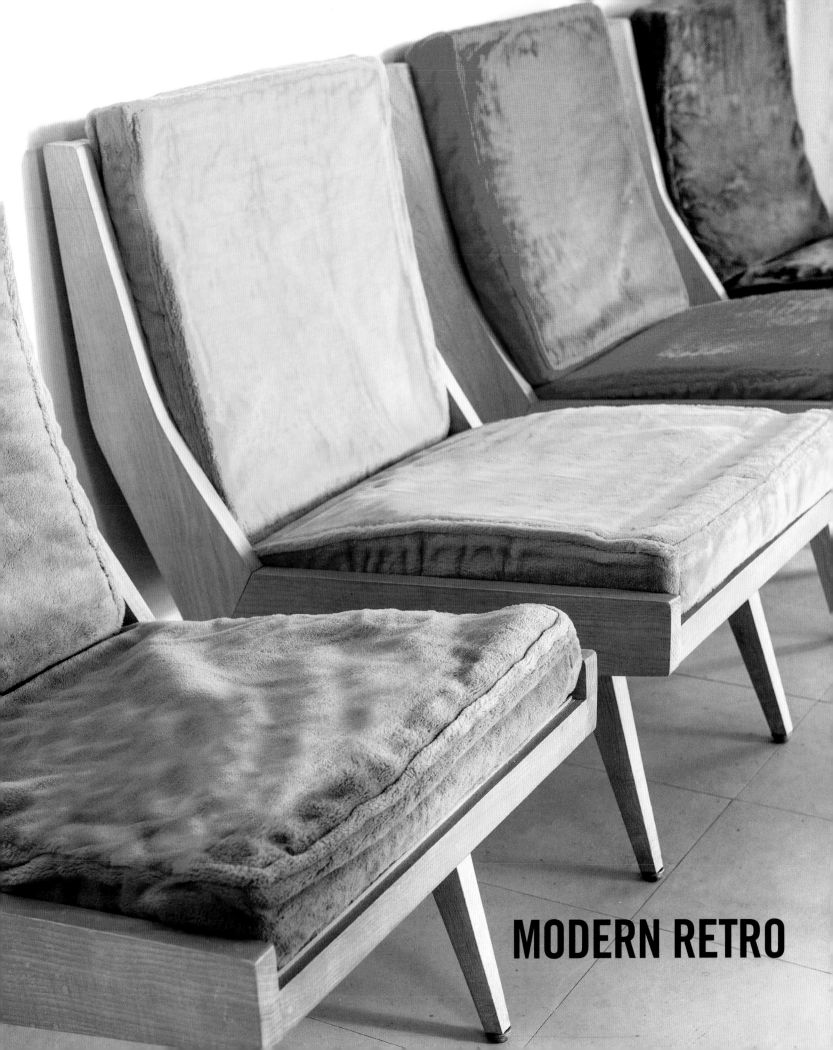

MODERN RETRO

CÔTÉ MAISON
MODERN RETRO
FROM RUSTIC TO URBAN, CLASSIC TO COLOURFUL

Caroline Clifton-Mogg

jacqui small

First published in 2016 by
Jacqui Small LLP
74–77 White Lion Street
London N1 9PF

Publisher: Jacqui Small
Managing Editor: Emma Heyworth-Dunn
Designer: Maggie Town
Editor: Sian Parkhouse
Production: Maeve Healy

ISBN: 978 1 910254 16 5

A catalogue record for this book is available from the British Library.

2018 2017 2016

10 9 8 7 6 5 4 3 2 1

Printed in China

Contents

Introduction
What is retro?

THIS BOOK takes a look at a fascinating design and decorative style – the first shoots of which, early modernism, emerged nearly one hundred years ago. It continued to grow for about forty years and still flourishes today, with many of the early designs looking as fresh and interesting as when they were first produced. But *Modern Retro* is not just about twentieth-century design – it is a book about how to work this wonderful style with new and contemporary design, as well as incorporating it with the vintage and the antique.

What exactly is retro? Even among people who really know about these things, there is a running debate as to what the term retro actually means in design language. There are some who think it means something from a short time ago, and others who see it as design from a specific period – somewhere vague centred between the 1920s and the 1970s. In vocabulary terms 'retro' is in fact a Latin prefix meaning backwards or in past times, and that seems to be the simplest way of looking at it ... distinguishing it from the antique, such as pieces from the eighteenth and nineteenth centuries.

Among the many consequences of the First World War was a growing feeling among a new generation of architects, designers and artists that there was another way to design – one in which function and practicality were as important as form, and where simplicity trumped decorative flourish. They found inspiration in the new technologies and techniques as well as new materials, many of which had been developed during the war but which were now explored in a domestic setting.

Central to the development of the movement was the Bauhaus, the school of architecture and design founded in Germany in 1919. Although it only lasted until 1933, when it was shut down by the Nazis, the Bauhaus

Right In Cornwall, a contemporary house with an interior that is a combination of the old and the new. The living space opens directly onto the garden, and the different living areas are unified by a ceiling in wood and a floor in oxidized stone. A giant-sized Lampadare floor lamp acts as a marker between the sitting area and the metal and wood reading table and its Thonet chairs.

Opposite The lines of twentieth-century furniture are timeless. In this Paris apartment, designed in the 1950s, much remains of the original layout, including this open shelving unit. The desk chair is a 1950s design by Pierre Guariche, and part of a collection of vintage Barbie dolls are the icing on the retro cake.

Below *In a kitchen of rough-hewn industrial charm kitchen detritus is hidden in sturdy wooden cupboards. Other elements include a very vintage, distressed metal table and classic metal chairs and oversized metal-shaded lamps hanging from the rafters.*

had an influence that stretched far beyond its gates and way beyond its years of life, and indeed still affects the furniture we buy today. The first director of the school was Walter Gropius, and other great designers such as Marcel Breuer and Ludwig Mies van der Rohe taught there; other designers who were influential at the time included Le Corbusier and Charlotte Perriand, Eileen Gray and Alvar Aalto and later Eero Saarinen, Isama Noguchi and Ray and Charles Eames – all famous names now but unknown then beyond a small group of like-minded designers and architects and design aficionados.

It is sometimes hard to realize just how revolutionary some of the early pieces must have seemed at the time; the combination of new techniques and new inventions resulted in materials with which we are very familiar today – bent tubular steel, moulded plastic and plywood – but which had never been seen before that period. Everything about the designs was new, which is perhaps one reason why so much early and mid-period twentieth-century furniture continues to be so popular today, and why it works so well in twenty-first-century interiors, as the homes in this book will amply demonstrate.

Below *Beneath beams of concrete, and on a floor of wide wooden boards a room of contrasts: antiques – a sofa, upholstered in velvet and a chair that has been de-upholstered back to its very roots – an ex-post office red-painted desk, a Bertoia chair, a 1950s lamp and a string-covered basket chair.*

RETRO STYLING

Creating the look

Below left *On one side of a dining area, separated from the kitchen by a wall and a simple hatch, an old wooden table with a set of Eero Saarinen Tulip chairs around it.*
Below centre *A 1920s house, restored to its former glory and given a new lease of life. In a corridor leading out to a terrace, a wire-framed chair designed by Warren Platner highlights the simplicity of the metal-framed doors.*

Below right *In a mountain chalet in Georgia, USA, a combination of the new and comfortable and retro design gives individuality to a bedroom.*
Opposite *A charming example of how retro-chic can work: a sideboard dating from the 1950s stands against a heavy stone wall; in front is a dining table, covered with a home-made collage of maps of the world, and two pairs of chairs. The connecting factor is that each piece has black, metal, angled legs.*

USING RETRO PIECES in a modern setting, or indeed a setting filled with styles of another period, is an exercise in style. Done well, retro-everything works with architecture of every period, from industrial spaces to rural retreats to eighteenth- and nineteenth-century nobly proportioned town houses; indeed, as many modern interior decorators have demonstrated, the clean elegant lines of eighteenth-century furniture married with equally elegant twentieth-century designs makes a harmonious marriage that is timeless.

Twentieth-century furniture, furnishings and accessories also work well in today's loft-inspired and ex-industrial open living areas. Much of the furniture was originally designed to be used in the new open-plan apartments that were seen as the future by architects such as Le Corbusier, who envisaged the end of single-purpose, single-function rooms. A new way of more informal living was the goal, so furniture was designed to be used in a more casual way – to be moved from area to area, if necessary, and perform in a multifunctional way; this means that many of these individual and sometimes standout pieces are more than happy to be placed in a larger space, where their individuality can be appreciated and admired.

You don't need many different pieces to enjoy retro style; in fact a case could be made – to quote Ludwig Mies van der Rohe – that less is more, in that some furniture and even some accessories punch well above their weight in terms of impact. The important thing to remember, as always in interior design and decoration of any period, is that the connecting thread is to make the right choices in the first place, work on clever and surprising combinations and always remember to employ thoughtful and disciplined editing.

In classic mode

The phrase 'classic retro' might almost seem a contradiction in terms, but it is of course a truism that every design that we now like to call 'classic' was at one time new and exciting – even Thomas Chippendale's designs would have seemed unusual and perhaps surprising to the Georgians as they studied his designs in The Gentleman and Cabinet Maker's Directory.

In our own century, the new classics in retro terms are those pieces from the leading designers and architects of the early to mid-twentieth century – names like Mies van der Rohe, Le Corbusier, Charlotte Perriand, Ray and Charles Eames, Eero Saarinen and Harry Bertoia. When first launched, pieces of furniture from these designers, and others like them, were rated by few – in fact, they were really only appreciated by the contemporary design community. Today, of course, they are highly collectable – both the original pieces, which are few and far between, as well as being extremely expensive, and the newer re-editions of the original designs made under licence.

Although many of these classic designs are now so familiar as to be almost unremarkable – apart from their ineffable air of class and style – at the time when they were first introduced, these new pieces were attempts by their designers (who in the main were architects) to introduce furniture that was not only different from what had gone before, but that would also complement their new modernist architecture designs. They wanted to showcase the new construction techniques that had been developed as well as many of the new finishes and materials such as fibreglass, chrome and rubber.

It was a design style that espoused clarity and simplicity and rejected the over-decorative and, as they saw it, over-elaborate applied ornament of earlier periods. Quality and attention to detail were inherent in the manufacture, and they were convinced that these designs would express the modern age. They do that, without doubt, but it is interesting that several of the pieces seem to have an affinity with furniture from antiquity – Mies van der Rohe's Barcelona chair seems to gently echo the lines of the Ancient Greek klismos chair, with its curved legs and angled back, as seen on artefacts and steles, and the elongated chaise longue of Le Corbusier seems to give more than a nod to the antique reclining couches of both the Ancient Greeks and Romans.

As we see them today, with the benefit of time and hindsight, these now-classic pieces display an elegance of design and form that sets them apart from many other retro

Opposite A pair of Bohemian quilted leather armchairs by Patricia Urquiado for Moroso in front of a low 1960s sideboard, the length of which accentuates the proportions of the room.
Below Against a corridor wall, furniture, objects and art from very different periods and in very different styles are united by the common denominator of colour – in this case, deep, glossy black.
Right A small corner is made significant through combining an antique desk, a shiny black Tulip chair by Eero Saarinen and a Napoleon III side table, dominated by an imposing photograph.

Left In a drawing room of classical proportions, complete with mouldings and cornices, are chairs and a daybed designed in the 1950s by Pierre Guariche. The low glass table is a design classic by Yves Klein.

Opposite, top left In a hallway framed by Corinthian columns is a New York chair with seat and back in woven brown leather strips.

Opposite, top right A library corner where opposites attract: an ornate, antique stove stands close to a Le Corbusier chaise longue, lit by a 1950s angled lamp. On the wall is a portrait of Richard Wagner, sculpted into the wall by the artist-owner.

Opposite, below Although lightly furnished, this room is very strong decoratively, assisted by the teal-blue colour of the original wall panelling, a clutch of armchairs from Paola Navone and versions of the Gras lamps strategically placed around the room.

styles. Often upholstered in leather, pony or cowskin, they have a confidence, born of provenance and strong beliefs, and although they are of the twentieth century, they more than hold their own in a room furnished with pieces from the eighteenth and nineteenth centuries – and indeed, the twenty-first. Married with earlier styles, they provide contrast, but also balance, proportion and scale, and, as can be seen looking at the rooms illustrated here, when these classic modernist pieces are used intelligently in an interior design scheme – that is, not just thrown into a room but chosen and placed with care – they add to the final mix, highlighting the qualities of the rest of the room, drawing out the best of the rest, so to speak. For when a design – any design – is good, it works with everything, with never a backward glance.

CASE STUDY STYLE SALON

Antiques dealer? Set designer? Decorator? Arnaud Caffort is all of the above. In his latest landing all his latest finds are for sale – which is good news for everyone.

Arnaud Caffort is a man of eclectic tastes. He is an admirer of the art and design of the twentieth century, the objects of his enthusiasm ranging from the work of artists like Andy Warhol and Keith Haring to the furniture designs of Ray and Charles Eames. And in his new apartment in Bordeaux he has pieces by all of the above as well as many others, but he not only owns them but sells them, too.

He moved, with his family, from a large space in Biarritz, in which he displayed his antique stock, to a large classically designed nineteenth-century apartment in Bordeaux, facing a public park. In this space lives not only his family but also his collection, and the way that he has displayed them is a lesson in interior arrangement. Each room is actually more like an art installation than a domestic interior, and yet the rooms are also surprisingly comfortable and easy to live in.

Opposite Fine nineteenth-century parquet flooring is a background for a diamond-patterned rug from Ikea, on which is set a low, 1970s coffee table and an unusual pair of Eva chairs by Swedish designer Bruno Mathsson from the 1970s.
Above The classical façade of the building in Bordeaux in which Arnaud Caffort has his large airy apartment.
Above right In the hall, a riot of colour and design: a Cassina re-edition of a 1918 Gerrit Rietveld Red/Blue chair, with a yellow perforated metal park bench. The bookcase, with a collection of Toucan nightlights, was designed by Arnaud Caffort.
Right Another eclectic collection: the ornate mouldings of the room are countered by a group that combines a 1970s floor clock in bright lacquered orange with a nineteenth-century table clock in its ornate case, both surveyed by a sculpture of a coat dating from the 1970s.

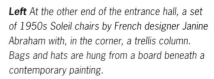

Left At the other end of the entrance hall, a set of 1950s Soleil chairs by French designer Janine Abraham with, in the corner, a trellis column. Bags and hats are hung from a board beneath a contemporary painting.
Below left A fine example of a typically 1950s sunray mirror, this one with rays of gilded wood.
Opposite The dining area with a rosewood dining table from the 1960s by Castiglioni and black and white Eames chairs from the 1950s. The heavy nineteenth-century wood chimneypiece is garnished with ceramics by Primavera, and the space is lit with hanging lights from Matthieu Lusterie.

In the entrance hall, for example, the original nineteenth-century mosaic floor in a stylized neoclassical design makes a background for a 1918-designed Gerrit Rietveld chair in the primary colours so associated with the early stages of modernism; the chair is in conversation with a bright yellow, contemporary, perforated metal park bench, the colour accentuated by a 1970s angled lamp on the windowsill, presided over by a bookcase designed by Arnaud. At the other end of the hall is a trio of Soleil rattan and metal chairs and their matching table, designed in the 1950s by Janine Abraham. Above them all hangs an armillary sphere light.

The family dining area is an equally interesting grouping of the unlikely with the improbable: in the centre of the space a classic mid-century rosewood table is teamed with black and white Eames chairs from the same period, the whole group dominated by a heavy, carved wood chimneypiece, furnished with books and ceramics and a contemporary painting, in place of the traditional mirror.

All these are unusual combinations, to say the least, which Arnaud orchestrates in masterly fashion. Although he makes it look simple to put such different periods and styles together and to show that everything coexists, it requires at the very least an exceptionally good eye and understanding of scale. It also requires confidence, which he obviously has in spades.

CASE STUDY

PARISIAN ELEGANCE

A soaring glass roof projects from the Parisian apartment home of an Italian art expert, bringing the city closer. Like a panoramic trompe-l'oeil, the symmetry of the neighbouring windows are brought into this space like a giant painting, next to contemporary works of art.

The moment you walk into the apartment you are struck by the light, and as you look out of the tall glass windows your eye is drawn to the stone façades of nineteenth-century Paris opposite, their presence imposing itself on the room. The room is high, with a mezzanine; the apartment is the perfect setting for the collection of modern and contemporary art belonging to Chiara Monteleone-Travia, a 34-year-old player on the contemporary art scene.

Taught by her father, a knowledgeable collector, whom she accompanied as a child to auction rooms and galleries, Chiara developed a flair for collecting beautiful things. In France, where she studied law, the young Milanese refined

Opposite This Parisian apartment is filled with light thanks to the wall of windows. The black-and-white composition that is the punctiliously arranged collection of signature pieces of furniture includes the curved chair and footstool designed by Sven Ellekaer in the 1950s and, either side of the window, an Eames Lounge chair in white leather and an Egg chair by Arne Jacobsen.

Below left On the chimney breast, a steel sculpture by Benoit Lemercier and, to the right, a series of pictures by Lee Bae.

Below right To one side of the chimney breast is a Lemercier daybed by Kerstin Hörlin Homlqvist.

her knowledge, encouraged by her husband, and inspired by two portraits by the celebrated Brazilian artist Vik Muniz that were the first fruits of their mutual addiction.

As well as contemporary art, Chiara has been collecting key – iconic, even – pieces of twentieth-century furniture, much of it bought from specialist dealer Florence Lopez, so she needed a space that would illuminate both strands of her collecting passion.

When Chiara found this apartment, it was far from the homogenous space it is today. It looked out of date, its aesthetics those of the 1980s, and Chiara felt that it needed bringing into the present. She therefore commissioned the architect Etienne Herpin to interpret what she wanted and suggest some new perspectives on the space. The existing mezzanine and staircase were to be transformed, their shapes softened and smoothed out so that the whole would come to reference the curved lines of 1930s architecture.

While creating a slightly vertiginous feeling to the room, a glass balustrade on the mezzanine floor added strong perspectives to the overall space and increased the sense of volume. Now a height of nearly 6m (20ft) means that the entire area has become a light-filled, deep space, where the white walls, the reflections of the glass and the graphic lines of the architecture all combine to make endless luminous variations on a theme.

Away from this spectacular central area, the private spaces are furnished with soft tones. 'I wanted the apartment to become almost a perfect box, a frame, where I could place the works and the furniture in a clear, uncluttered way where they could stand and be appreciated in an unconfused way,' Chiara explains. The plan succeeded and the paintings, sculptures, photographs and furniture combine to take possession of the space and to make the whole apartment a homogenous artistic experience.

Right In the small sitting room below the mezzanine, a large painting by Farah Atassi looms over a sinuous chaise longue, FK87 Grasshopper by Preben Fabricius and Jorgen Kastholm, and a pumpkin-like top-sitched black leather pouffe from Poltrona Frau.

Opposite, left The master bedroom is a pearl-grey haven with a chair by Fornasetti in the window, bedside tables from the 1940s and, on the wall, a classic sunburst mirror.

Opposite, right In the office, a rug by Christopher Farr sets the tone, with chairs by Bertoia running beneath a built-in double desk-top.

CASE STUDY
CONTEMPORARY CLASSIC

For two years now, Manfred Geserick, whose Paris apartment is in Montorgueil, not far from Les Halles, has thrown himself into his quest to create a perfect, and particular home.

The apartment is on the second floor of one of those peculiarly French buildings – a nineteenth-century *hôtel particulier* – the generic name for the grand, usually detached, old town mansions peculiar to some French cities. The space and proportions therefore are generous – two reception rooms, a dining room, kitchen and a bedroom with a small terrace, certainly room to create the perfect Parisian décor.

Dutch by birth, and an enthusiastic globetrotter, moving between Italy, Portugal and France, Manfred Geserick, a creative fashion designer and consultant, uses his travels as much for design influences as for inspiration for his collections, all of which is reflected in his transformation of his new living space, where he juggles with styles, bringing a modernity and a new life to this classical space. 'I wanted to simplify the spaces, while keeping their original grandeur,' he says. The first thing he did was to open up the rooms, making them work together, in order to take full advantage of the daylight. He wanted to emphasize the bones of the space – the ceilings, parquet floors, beams and moulding – working with them as a showcase for his pieces of contemporary furniture and art.

'My idea was to subtly introduce changes of period, to bring the rooms into the atmosphere of the twenty-first century, where I could mix and combine the unlikely and unusual. I want to create a tension between styles and periods, to move away from the idea of pure design, which on its own can become impersonal and boring.'

In the salon, a fine room with original wood parquet flooring in a herringbone pattern, Manfred has contrasted the rather solemn architecture with a long, low sofa designed in the 1970s and covered in acid-green velvet; two chairs from the 1950s sit opposite, and above the stone fireplace hangs an eighteenth-century mirror. It takes a sure eye to combine such opposites with success.

In the library there are other interesting connections: within a striking framework of grey-painted, nineteenth-century panelling and a fine brick-lined, stone fireplace,

Left *A dining room of surprises with, on the original herring-bone parquet floor, a table by Knoll, with bentwood classic chairs by Thonet. Above hangs an airy chandelier, originally from L'Hôtel de la Tremoille in Paris. At one side of the room, built-in shelves display a catholic group of objects and surround a high-backed, velvet-covered banquette that surveys the whole scene.*
Opposite *A sure eye has put together this group of contrasts, where a Louis XV mirror above the fireplace holds together a group that includes a pair of 1950s chairs found at a flea market, and a low, leather-covered table, made by the apartment's owner, Manfred Geserick.*

Right *This side of the salon has an oversized, gilded frame as a counterpoint to the eighteenth-century mirror above the fireplace. The frame runs the length of the sofa, which dates from the 1970s. Throughout the apartment, the original, lightly restored, wooden flooring laid in a simple herring-bone design, acts as a stylistic reference point. The contrast between the acid tones of the furnishings and the neutral ones of the background is striking.*

Above left Ornamented with nineteenth-century wooden panelling, both the screen and the bookcases in the library have been painted in harmonious tones of grey. Strong contrast comes between the sofas, which have been covered in raw linen, and the astrakhan cushions.
Above right Beneath a wall made up of antique mirror glass, mounted with a pair of old candle-holding sconces, is an uncompromisingly modern armchair from B&B Italia.
Opposite The dining room, with its ceiling of old beams and parquet floor, is a dramatic space, containing a Knoll table, Thonet chairs and a drop chandelier from a hôtel particulier. On the wall, a photo by François Rousseau is hung next to a work of Michael van den Besselaar. An eclectic group indeed!

Manfred has introduced grey linen-covered sofas and chairs (dressed with astrakhan cushions that he made from old coats) with a close-hung collection of pictures and drawings, ranging from French pastels to Ukranian icons and nineteenth-century Italian paintings.

In the dining room he has combined an exuberant, low-hung chandelier with a glass table by Knoll and classic Thonet bentwood chairs that he bought from a hotel in the Auvergne.

Much of the restoration Manfred has done himself in a little studio on the same floor that he has fitted out as the perfect workshop and where he cuts, sands, welds and assembles. This practical dexterity is seen in the kitchen, where he designed the granite work surface. Facing this are three silvered columns suspended above the floor and which hold the ovens, fridge and dishwasher.

The whole apartment illustrates a creativity that makes one long to have the skill to be one's own decorator, for the charm of this very Parisian space comes from a subtle alchemy of elegance, curiosities and surprises on every level.

Rustic reclamation

Rustic Retro is an interesting exercise in how the recognizable elements of rustic architecture – which, by its very definition, is usually found in the country and is more often than not a working building that has been converted for domestic living – combine so very well with the often sharper angles of quirky and sometimes modernist twentieth-century furniture and objects.

The recognizably rustic is an architectural style much admired by many. It is a celebration of construction and of an everyday hard-working life, and those who restore such spaces usually do so by exposing, rather than concealing, the bones of a building, for it is these bones, the skeleton, that give the homes their character. The rough-and-ready nature of many rustic or rural interiors lends itself well to reclamation retro – against local materials and raw beams, the forms of mid-century furniture stand out in sharp relief.

These rooms, these spaces, have an instant patina, a sense of age and purpose, and a setting that offers few furbelows and little extra ornament. The stripped-back environment means that when you introduce furniture and objects they must not only respect the architecture and personality of the place, as well as fulfil a practical purpose, but they must also add several missing elements to the final mix. Comfort, definitely. Individual personality, hopefully, and perhaps even pleasure – for rustic living will not work if the architecture is allowed to take over and dominate.

In these interiors there may well be stone – lots of it, possibly on the floor or the walls, or both, and often left bare. Plaster can be rough, rather than polished, and sometimes left in its natural state, rather than coloured. And everywhere there will be wood – again, perhaps, on the floor, and often in beams and

Left In an old drying-house under the roof, a section of a kitchen-dining room. The rustic elements – the bare stone wall, the raw beams and the natural oak floorboards – are close at hand. The metal table from Axel-Olivier Icard and the vintage metal chairs by Tolix work perfectly against the rough setting.

Left A steel cooking range has been turned into something rather glamorous beneath an extractor fan and hood disguised in an ornate old chimney canopy.

Below The rusticity of this restored stone house has been complemented by the natural colours and tones used in the furnishings: natural linen on the sofas and cushions in tones that echo the building materials, and a low table made of rough planks on a scaffold-like metal base.

rafters, which by their very nature can be heavy and sometimes
almost overwhelming in appearance. (Although, conversely,
if they are vertical – embedded into the wall or a structural
beam set mid-floor – beams can become a decorative element
to be played up, rather than played down.) These architectural
stalwarts are texture, but texture in the raw, and they need to be
softened by the complementary texture that comes from textiles
and soft furnishings – cushions, pillows and comfortable chairs,
rugs and quilts and even the odd curtain at a window or door.
These elements are essential in any once-working environment.

Colour is used as well to soften and humanize; not all-over,
all-round colour, perhaps, which would sanitize and negate the

surroundings, but injections of it to add warmth and contrast to what is, by its natural nature, usually a pretty neutral space.

Interestingly, the furniture of the twentieth century works particularly well in these spaces because it is chameleon-like and adaptable. Neither antique nor über-contemporary, the materials used to make these twentieth-century pieces work better than anything else with the natural textures of the surrounding space; metal, polished wood, moulded plastic and fibreglass have their own semi-organic appearance that blends happily into the mix. What is important is that the furniture and objects chosen should have minds of their own – no shrinking violets, but no flashy sunflowers either.

Below *Both kitchen and sitting room share this very large convivial living area. Along the outside wall is the cooking area and the dining table, while a comfortable seating area is made from a curved-arm sofa and a pair of vintage Steiner armchairs, found through a listing in the classified ads in the local newspaper.*

CASE STUDY NORMANDY WORKSHOP

Ivory Coast in West Africa? Or Alabaster Coast in Normandy? In fact this conversion is a bit of both! Monique Chicot, a textile artist and a native of Fécamp in Normandy, and her husband, who was born in Senegal, West Africa, have renovated what was once a four-floored furniture workshop in Fécamp into a quirky and genuinely eclectic interior.

The building, which dates from the start of the twentieth century, was originally four levels of work rooms stretching over 320m² (3,444 square feet). When it came to renovating and restoring the complex area and making it into a comfortable living space, Monique Chicot knew that they must create a suitable background for displaying and, in some cases, using, the many African pieces – sculptures and furniture – that they had collected over time. And it was a considerable time – Monique had lived in Africa for twenty-five years; the continent had made an indelible impression on her, and she wanted not only to enjoy her collections at their best but also to incorporate some of the tones, textures – and, indeed, atmosphere – of the place she had loved for so long.

All good restoration projects respect the purpose and architecture of the original space; this job was no different. Monique and her husband were careful to reference in each room the industrial inheritance of the space: lime-washed stone walls, exposed beams and brick surfaces, anthracite-

Above The restored workshop building with the two new floors added by Monique Chicot.

Opposite The first-floor living room, which looks over the street. On the left is a steamer chair with arms, which originated from the transatlantic liner France. There are African touches everywhere in the room are: by the sofa, a pair of stools, and on the opposite wall, a pair of 30s-style armchairs, all from the Ivory Coast.

Right In the kitchen, the floor has been restored, and a new kitchen from Ikea now runs along one wall. In the centre is an antique worktable with vintage bistro chairs set around it. On the wall is one of Monique Chicot's own paintings.

Above left On the wall, a large picture by Monique, above a wooden chair made in the Ivory Coast, with a painting by Jean-Marc Louis. Beside the chair, a column supports a sculpture of twisted vegetable fibres from Chad.
Above right Under the original staircase of the building is a Malinke bench. Further along is the now restored old fireplace.
Opposite One end of the space is used as a study, where African objects are combined with contemporary furniture, a set of industrial shelving and a free-form floor lamp of curved and twisted metal.

coloured woodwork, as well as original floorboards that were painted or polished. These back-to-basics elements are balanced by the confident slashes of strong colour: oxblood-red in the bathroom, acid-green in the kitchen, golden yellow in the hall. These are all colours that can be seen in the textiles and surroundings of West Africa, and which form a further contrast with not only the furniture but also with Monique's art, which is, in the main, in tones that are deep, almost sombre – earth and mineral tones.

The furniture that fills – or, rather, doesn't fill – the rooms is in keeping with the uncompromising industrial background of the space. Many of the pieces are from Africa and, in particular, the Ivory Coast: heavy wooden chairs, squat wooden stools, low tables and a pair of scooped-out armchairs like hammocks of wood. These are combined with more European finds: a draper's wooden table in the kitchen, old bistro chairs and – stylish and romantic – a cushioned wooden armchair, that once did service on the legendary transatlantic liner the *France*. The lighting, in contrast, is contemporary, which is a perfect foil for the ethnic and the old.

All in all, these crosscurrents, changes of mood, tempo and cultures, have been most skilfully brought together in a *tour de force* of careful selection and very clever design.

CASE STUDY STRIPPED-BACK COUNTRY

The village of Lyons-la-Forêt, one of the most beautiful in Normandy, revels in a surfeit of charming, seventeenth-century, half-timbered, pink brick houses. Cyrille and Julie Viard's plan was to reinterpret the genre – adding a touch of industrial fantasy to the traditional charm.

In the heart of the magnificent and imposing beech national forest of Lyons, stands the village of Lyons-la-Forêt, a perfectly preserved, half-timbered Norman village, and nowhere is the charm more pronounced than on the eighteenth-century central Place des Halles, so quintessentially French that it served as the setting for the making of not one, but two, films of Gustave Flaubert's novel *Madame Bovary* (the first made by Jean Renoir in 1932, the second by Claude Chabrol in 1990). As cinema fans, this was yet another reason for Cyrille and Julie Viard, owners of the decorating business L'Empreinte, to make their home here.

The story began when Cyrille, who had spent his childhood in the village, decided after ten years of living in Paris to come back to the region and to rebuy his childhood home, which stood on the edge of the ancient beech forest. Unsurprisingly, the layout and design of the house needed a complete

Above In front of the wisteria-covered old farmhouse are metal chairs and a round table from the 1950s.
Right The room has been opened up to reveal the old staircase where the metal steps and rail have been replaced with oak. The sofa is covered with an old quilt, in front of which is a table from the 1950s. Behind an old work bench next to the door is a group of etchings and watercolours by Jean Hulin.

Opposite On the other side of the now opened room, divided by beams, the kitchen is dominated by a vintage table used for food preparation and eating, with vintage metal chairs from the 1950s on either side. The glazed kitchen door leads out into the garden and the summer dining room.

Right In a corner bound by beams, a small child's chair and an armchair from the 1950s. The hanging lights are electric glass isolators, making a contemporary mobile. On the wall, portraits of Julie's family and ink drawings by Alain Bonnefoit.

Below right In a small study, below one of the original windows, a Napoleon III desk, found in a grocer's shop in Lyons. Early twentieth-century stools and a metal wall lamp add to the working atmosphere. On the wall is a collection of witches' mirrors.

rethink, and before long they had upturned the house from top to bottom. Like so many old, small houses, the narrow windows and small rooms made the interior darker than might have been wished, so Cyrille and Julie decided to open up the rooms, wherever possible, to maximize what daylight there was. Of course, with an old house, the structural beams, both horizontal and vertical, could not be removed, so on the ground floor they took down the wall between the living room and the kitchen, leaving just the beautiful, rough-textured beams. Suddenly the space was opened up and illuminated, and so Cyrille and Julie went further, stripping back the cob wall finish to reveal the original brick, and the beams, once painted, were stripped back and then patinated.

As well as a living room, there is a study and a small book room. The kitchen, which opens onto the living room, is organized around a large table and industrial metal chairs; a glazed door – another device to increase natural light – leads into the garden and a summer dining room. An open staircase, with treads of oak, leads up to the bedrooms – an enfilade of simple rooms, beneath the rafters, with open beams and walls gently tinted with chalk paint.

Cyrille and Julie have used a clever combination of the slightly industrial and the slightly rural, softening the metal and wood, both upstairs and down, with fat cushions and quilts. Drawings, watercolours and paintings, many of them by Julie's grandfather, Jean Hulin, are hung on walls and up the stairs. The mood is relaxed and comfortable – and perfectly in keeping with the unique atmosphere of the ancient village.

Structural industrial

An interesting and strong area of architectural and interior design over the last few decades – particularly in towns and cities – has been the reclamation and reconfiguration of workshops, factories and warehouses, the urban version of converted barns and farms, to redesign them into comfortable and often very striking living spaces. And – on the whole – very successful the process has been, too.

Many of these original buildings, of course, have wonderful proportions – designed for machinery and for workers and their tools, they are often airy and light, while retaining a sense of bulk and solidity, and because the area was once designed to contain machines and men, there is enough physical space to create both a sense and a reality of fluid movement and easy circulation.

Whether you think of these conversions as structural or industrial, it is important to respect the spirit of the place in the design of a new domestic environment, and in the very best of these new/old spaces, there is always a hard-edged element within the space, the overall theme being dominated by the materials, which are mostly those of the factory or workshop. With that in mind, the contemporary schemes that work best are those that retain the feeling of a working building, a sense of others' working lives, incorporating elements like metal window frames and doors, solid structural beams – sometimes wooden, but also sometimes of steel or iron – and often the original floor. In the most successful of these conversions, emphasis is laid on the colour or finish

Left *Restoration in an entrance hall leading into the living area: everything from the metal-framed windows to the tiled floor and even the radiator. The colour scheme in various shades of grey pulls everything together.*
Opposite *Restoring an industrial space can be immensely rewarding, particularly if you emphasize its past, while giving it a stylish present. A kitchen, part of a larger living area, is a shining combination of metal, limed wood and cement (in the tiles). Chic and graphic, and surprisingly welcoming too.*

of the industrial side of things: the metal window frames and structural beams are painted black or grey, the floors are left in the original or relaid with tile or solid planks of wood that mirror the originals, and rugs or carpets are conspicuous by their absence. Also lacking is anything other than the simplest of window coverings. And quite right too – these spaces are not for frilly cushions and floral drapes!

On the furniture front, semi-industrial pieces – metal filing cabinets used for storage, open-sided metal shelving, old store fittings re-utilized in diverse ways, work benches converted into more domestic working surfaces or tables, and wooden pallets made into low coffee and side tables – find a natural resting place in these spaces.

This does not mean that all the furniture and objects chosen for these converted spaces should be industrial in origin, but neither should they be too lightweight, and certainly not metaphorically fluffy. A contrast is what works best, coupled with a discernible element of comfort, particularly in the seating choices – fat 1950s upholstered armchairs and sofas are always welcome in these once working environments. In this sort of setting self-confident retro pieces come into their own, manufactured, as they were, using new techniques and new materials – think moulded plastic and moulded plywood. Straight from the factory floor, one might say.

Generally speaking, the colours that work best in these spaces are those that continue to reference the origins of the building, which means neutral walls – often white – with colour added not from paint, but from pictures and objects on the walls, as there is usually more than enough space on which to hang oversized and often imposing works.

It goes without saying that lighting, even if not entirely industrial in design, seems to work best if it nods to industrial tradition, although the occasional, larger-than-life chandelier can have a surprisingly decorative impact against these rigorously edited backgrounds.

Opposite A glass wall that separates a small reading and sitting room from a kitchen was designed after the unusual light fitting – Milk Bottle by Droog design – was installed on the floor. Old family furniture has been combined with modern pieces, including a pair of stools from Tolix.
Above right An ex-work space has been converted into a light-filled living room. The table and matching benches, designed in industrial mode by Ben Higgins, are African mahogany and aluminium. A very '60s touch is the elongated lamp by Kundalini.
Right Simple lines: ironwork against blond stone and old wood shutters, which have been remade in the traditional way.

Left The working corner of the apartment is enlivened by a collection of vinyl LPs and a pinball table surface is set into the frame of a door.
Opposite The living area of Stuart Haygarth's loft, with a pleasing combination of the vintage and the new, the latter represented by sofas designed by Hella Jongerius and chairs by Ronan and Erwan Bouroullec. The coffee table is on wheels, as is the converted standard lamp. A vintage light hangs from the ceiling, and a large wood-burning stove fits in well with the overall theme.

CASE STUDY FACTORY OF FOUND OBJECTS

A collector of vintage pieces, the sculptor Stuart Haygarth keeps all his finds in his London loft. It is an artist's den of furniture and their stories.

Stuart Haygarth is an artist – a sculptor and a craftsman – who designs and makes pieces using and reusing collections of *objets trouvés*, which can range from the glass from old pairs of prescription spectacles to see-through plastic wine glasses and kitsch plastic pieces from pound shops. Nothing is lost, everything is transformed. This is the formula that informs his work – sculptures of the functional. Light fittings are an area which inspires him and where he is tirelessly inventive – one spectacular chandelier in a public building in Ipswich was concocted from thirty-six tutus from the Russian Ballet, and other pieces have been created from flotsam found on the beach. As he says, 'My work is about giving the banal and overlooked objects a new significance.'

Right An overview of the apartment, with its stainless-steel kitchen. The dining table is lit with eleven low-hanging, tulip-shaped Carnival glass lamps from the 1920s, each one slightly different in design.

Perhaps luckily, his own home, where he lives with his partner Melanie Mangot, a photographer, and their daughter Billie, is not quite so extreme, yet it is filled with examples of pieces and furniture that espouse the idea of recycling and restoring. The apartment is a large space in what was formerly a factory in Shoreditch in the East End of London, and Stuart has elected to retain the existing industrial metal structure, including the window frames – which are painted a soft green rather than the more obvious black – and supporting pillars (also green), as well as the exposed wooden beams and the original floor of mellow oak boards.

The space has been kept open, which means that it is flooded with light, and the area has been divided into zones corresponding to different work and living areas. Running along one wall is the kitchen work space, which segues nicely into a dining area. Around the long dining table is a friendly combination of vintage chairs; it is lit with a pleasing group of suspended mismatched tulip-shaped lamps of coloured glass dating from the 1920s. On the other side of the room is a relaxed, large sitting area, which leads into an office-study space with a desk set beneath another large window. Around the staircase leading to the ground floor, Stuart has built bookcases from old sets of shelving. The furniture is a pleasing combination of the quite old and the very new, with vintage cabinets and sideboards rubbing shoulders with sofas and chairs that are the work of contemporary designers. The impression is one of a laid-back, yet very confident style that takes every find not at its face value but as a hidden treasure with infinite possibilities.

Opposite A swing suspended from the overhead beam delineates the sitting area from the working end of the room and adds to the playful atmosphere.

Above Above the staircase, a reading chair in moulded red plastic and chrome is practically placed next to the recycled bookcases crammed with reading material.

Left La Collongue in the Luberon, once a farm and magnanerie, where silkworms were cultivated, is now a sympathetically restored airy home and guesthouse.
Below left and right The building has been restored in a manner that allows the natural materials and original contours of the place to speak for themselves. Here, the hall and open staircase lead to the four bedrooms above. The walls and ceiling have been lime-washed in sand tones.

CASE STUDY WHITEWASHED WALLS

A longing to live life at a gentler pace resulted in Guillaume Toutain transforming an old working farm in the Luberon into Maison Collongue – a small bed and breakfast hotel as well as a dream home.

Lourmarin is a small commune in the Luberon, a popular area of Provence. For some years, Guillaume Toutain, a creative director based in Paris, had dreamed of settling 'in the south, somewhere calm, somewhere green'. In Lourmarin, at the intersection of two tributaries of the River Luberon, he found his haven: a traditional building that was part-agricultural and part-domestic. It was, he says, 'Like a childhood dream, I was finally about to be able to lead my own project, after always having worked on projects for others.'

The building had originally been, like others in this part of France, a silkworm farm and was made up of a working building dating from the seventeenth and eighteenth centuries

This page Furnishing the space was done with the help of local antique dealer Charlotte Olofgörs, who brought her own brand or retro style to the house. In the hall, a free-standing bookcase from the 1960s, a re-edition in white of the Eames's La Chaise and an abstract-patterned rug from the 1970s.

This page Twentieth-century furniture design works so well in these simple, vaulted ceiling rooms. The dining table is Danish, designed in 1958 by Svante Skogh. Mis-matched chairs are designs by Eames and Arne Jacobsen.

adjoining a later, nineteenth-century farmhouse. After nine months of work, the entire area was transformed. Like a white wave, walls were restored and lime-washed, spaces redistributed and reconfigured. Everything was brought together – the two halves united by a room in the form of a library to make a Provençal space that is contemporary yet aware of its history.

Guillaume's plan was to have one part of the building as his personal living quarters, the other part as an intimate and special bed and breakfast. This side of the building included a large salon, the ceiling of which seems to stretch up into infinity. There is a beautiful and practical professional kitchen, a well-proportioned dining room and an airy hall from where an open staircase rises towards four bedrooms. On the ground floor, the vaulted walls and ceilings are coloured in sand tones, while the first floor has walls of a pure white, which spreads across the dados, mouldings and ceilings.

Once the major work was finished, the next phase could begin, and the question was how to furnish the space without breaking it up and destroying the calm of the design; Guillaume's intent was to 'be radical with perfect aesthetics'. By happy chance, the antique dealer Charlotte Olofgörs had just brought in her collection of vintage pieces to the village, transposed from her other gallery in neighbouring Bonnieux. For Guillaume, this was a serendipitous moment and between this devotee of design and art and the specialist in Scandinavian design, there was an immediate understanding. From Charlotte's store they sourced clean-lined, simple chairs, armchairs, tables and banquettes. Together they organized the arrangement of rooms – here, a dresser by Omann Junior from the 1960s, there, a sofa in sky blue wool by Johannes Andersen, a carpet by Ryor and art-prints and etchings, all Scandinavian in origin. Thus the style 'Collongue' took shape, a style that works in every season, both inside and out, where, in summer, guests breakfast and dine beneath the lime trees, for Guillaume now also provides beautiful breakfasts and divine dinners. Definitely, the good life on the road to Collongue.

Above right The bedrooms are as calm as the reception rooms. Here, white cotton curtains are hung on a painted pole, and the room is furnished with vintage pieces and a striking Scandinavian rug in tones of bright yellow.
Right An open storage cabinet, typical of mid-century design, holds the china and glass in the dining area. Strongly shaped Scandinavian ceramics are grouped on top.

CASE STUDY

URBAN BOHEMIAN

Architect Karine Striga's house in the busy city of Marseille is an unexpected surprise. Set in a verdant garden, it is an oasis of peace in an urban area.

It is unusual, and indeed surprising, in such a busy city as Marseille, where change and modernization are all around, to find a house so of its time – that time being the nineteenth century – and so preserved, although without a touch of aspic in the recipe. When Karine Striga bought the house she realized at once that there was much former glory that could quite easily be revived – albeit with a lot of energy, as well as a touch of boldness; there were century-old parquet floors to be sanded, ceramic tiles to be repaired and polished, mouldings to be restored, walls to be painted. Although any one of these tasks might prove daunting to an ordinary mortal, nothing here posed any problem to Karine – with a diploma from the Ecole Nationale Supérieure d'Architecture de Marseilles, and having already practised her gift for renovation in a light-filled loft in the south of the city, she was well qualified to deal with such mundane practical matters, as well as to create an atmosphere of harmony throughout the house.

The finished house is a quirky mixture of whimsical charm and industrial chic, put together with a light touch; and as in all the best interior design, the conventional has been shaken up, and even stirred a bit. In the large living room, for example – a fine example of a nineteenth-century French town house salon – the restored wall panelling frames the imposing, original marble fireplace, and the tall windows are curtained, not in silks or velvets, but in light and frothy white cotton. As a counterbalance, a bright red Eames chair from the 1950s sits happily with

Opposite *A classic nineteenth-century building on a leafy Marseille street hides a surprising and eclectic melange of design, new and old.*
Left *The high-ceilinged living room is furnished with confidence; two mismatched, sofas are covered in rough natural cotton. The low tables, found at a local flea market, are converted storage palettes. In front of the original, ornate fireplace is a bright red, moulded plastic Eames chair on rockers from the 1940s. The scheme is set off by heavy curtains in perforated cotton and a fantasy hanging light of birds in a mesh cage.*
Below *The entrance hall, with its ornate ornamental mouldings, is home to an accomplished combination of images and mirrors. Heavy rectangular gilt-framed mirrors and collages of photographs are grouped with circular frames and a sunray mirror.*

cotton-covered sofas and low, no-nonsense tables that have been made from wooden pallets. The whimsical element is provided by the hanging pendulum light in the form of an airy, metal-barred birdcage, complete, of course, with bright-coloured birds, and the calligraphy that runs the length of a panel on one side of the fireplace. It reads 'Walls have ears …'

In the kitchen the sense of industrial, working life is strong, but still combined with shots of wit and whimsy. Cool white-lacquered units stand out against grey metal storage – one an oversized chest that has definitely seen filing cabinet duty in a former life. Grey-painted walls and stone work surfaces contrast with clear Perspex stools from the Marseille flea market. There are charming and original touches, such as the upside-down white porcelain teacups suspended above the worktop that happily masquerade as lights; there is also small wall cupboard that Karine has papered in several sheets of old Chinese newspapers. As Karine herself says, 'In this house, everything is easy.'

Opposite and above left *The large kitchen, with both eating areas and working areas, is decorated and furnished in cool colours, with grey walls, heavy, metal vintage industrial storage cabinets and white-lacquered units from Castorama with stone work surfaces. Vintage Plexiglass stools, moulded plastic chairs and a metal office stool make for varied seating. Hanging above the central island unit are lights in the form of oversized, inverted, white porcelain teacups.*
Above right *On top of the metal filing cabinet and below an unusual modern wall clock is a pleasing collection of old carafes and decanters dating from the nineteenth and twentieth centuries.*

CASE STUDY LIGHT INDUSTRIAL

When it comes to design, antique dealers Michel Peraches and Eric Miele do not lack imagination, and imaginative industrial chic is their style of choice.

Both Michel and Eric, who are antique dealers in the Market Paul Bert in Saint-Ouen, Paris, are familiar with industrial buildings – it is their favoured area of design, and in Paris they have converted several such buildings into striking loft apartments. 'We like to respect the site and we believe in trying to revive the original spirit of the place and also to retain a part of Paris that is fast disappearing.'

The apartment on these pages, however, was not for a client, but for themselves. They have found a space in the heart of the 11th arrondissement in Paris, the top floor of a large building that once held furniture makers' workshops, and here they have created an apartment that is airy and light-filled, which has not lost the spirit of its past; it now breathes again with a contemporary air, and is as comfortable and warm as one could wish.

The original structure, the framework of solid industrial beams and metal-framed windows, was the basis for their

Opposite *The structural beams of this industrial space play a large part in the arrangement and design of the living area, and the space is furnished accordingly in a mixture of styles, each piece strong enough to stand on its own. A contemporary sofa from Caravane, a Barcelona chair by Mies van der Rohe and an angled Gras floor lamp, designed in 1922, all play their part.*
Above *The industrial framework of the original building, both the exterior and the interior, has been preserved and restored.*
Above right *A parquet floor from a ballroom was recycled, restored and relaid here and now runs through the whole space. The low table is made from recycled wooden pallets and matches the mood.*
Right *The glass bays with their iron frames and the massive structural beams are constant reminders of the ateliers that once were widespread in the area. The whole space benefits enormously from daylight.*

renovation. 'We wanted to rework the space, to restore the feeling of these old working buildings, and create within the apartment a feeling of space and a sense of fluid movement and easy circulation throughout, as well as providing views from every side. We have created a large living space with metal-framed glass bays that echo the design of the old workshops.' Around this living space are linked the kitchen, the office, the bathroom and the principal bedroom. Uniting the originally separate spaces is a terrace, framed with metal panels, that leads out from the glass walls of the living space and overlooks the inner court of the building.

The original space was broken into five separate workshops; uniting them gave Michel and Eric a chance to bring together their large personal – and eclectic – collection

Above In the kitchen area of the living space, an industrial look prevails, with dark grey wooden and metal work units and island units, lit from above by glass hanging lamps from Emmanuel Ricci. A pair of moulded plastic chairs in dark red by Verner Panton add a flash of colour.

Opposite The beams in the dining area, as in the rest of the space, have been stained in a neutral khaki-grey. Beyond the dining table, sliding glass sections lead out onto a terrace furnished with Bertoia chairs. The simple dining table is surrounded with Marteau chairs by Arne Jacobsen, and headed with an Eames moulded plastic chair.

of art, lighting and furniture. The space is large enough to have given the pair great freedom to combine the different elements of their very extensive possessions. Among the pieces are military folding camp chairs and table, bright red moulded Verner Panton chairs, an eighteenth-century glass chandelier and low tables made from wooden palettes. There is industrial shelving and the curtains are made from antique sheets. Everything has a place and there is a place for everything.

To get such a mix right requires a broad understanding of proportion and an intuitive feeling for individual pieces. Without betraying its industrial past, Michel and Eric have succeeded in reinventing a space that is, in its essence, very contemporary and very Parisian in feel.

Left and above Leading from the bedroom is the office area of the space, both chair and desk are vintage designs from Jean Prouvé. The Gras lamp on the desk is an original, and the hanging light with its chrome shade is a design by Mario Mengotti.
Opposite The bedroom is as simply furnished as the rest of the apartment, with carefully chosen pieces of furniture. The bed with its studded headboard is supplemented by a LCW wooden chair designed in 1946 by Charles and Ray Eames.

Colourful

Colour has always been an essential element of interior design and architecture, both structurally and interms of furnishings and objects. The preferred palette at any time is as dependent on the vagaries of public taste as it is on the range of colours actually available.

Architects, of course, have long used colour as a tool, rather than just as a decorative add-on, and one of the most important of the twentieth-century designers who saw the potential of colour in ways that went far beyond simple decoration was the Swiss architect Le Corbusier, who viewed colour as a vital spatial device. He understood – and wrote – that colour in architecture was as important a tool as the ground plan of a building. So interested was he in the application of colour within the home that he developed two colour palettes for a Swiss paint company – the first in the

This page The wall of rough stone in this living area accentuates the flighty lightness of the bright red Pop-Up chairs that bring warmth into the space. A trio of vintage-coloured circular tables in lacquered wood and two 1960s armchairs add to the mix.

Opposite A small but perfect still life in colour. Against a bright red wall, a Verner Panton moulded plastic chair in purple and a stack of cushions are as ornamental as they are useful.

1930s and a second chart twenty years later including colours and neutrals that he was wont to use to create warmth, light, atmosphere and detail in his architectural projects. He wrote an incredibly detailed analysis on the use of colour and its functions, and his practical applications of his colour theories were extremely influential over the years, and remain so today.

The colour palette popular in the mid-twentieth century was bright and graphic – firstly because the development of ready-mixed synthetic paints had taken off during the second half of the century and the range of colours available had increased exponentially. And, secondly, because the 1950s were the age of the consumer – beneficiaries of a post-war boom in which, after the grey war years, there was a sense of returning confidence, which manifested itself in many ways, including home improvements. And that meant colour – the brighter the better. There were cheerful primaries, but also citrus tones – limes, lemons and oranges. All these shades were bright and sometimes hard, but compelling, strong and unmissable – and they were used with cheerful abandon throughout the house. Pastels were not rejected, but they also were bright – candy colours, sugar pink and baby blue. The age of distressed, colours and tones that were 'knocked back' was far in the future, so using this bright, unabashed palette in a modern interior does definitely bookmark the 1950s.

Open-plan living – or versions of it – was being espoused and put into practice by Le Corbusier and other architects of the time, and these larger spaces, rather than small, single-use rooms that had previously been a domestic staple, made the use of stronger colours even more acceptable; an arresting 'accent' wall was easy to live with in a space that encompassed several functions.

These larger, multifunctional living spaces brought about the introduction of a further design innovation, that of built-in and multifunctional pieces of furniture: storage walls, room dividers that doubled as book and storage space and, of course, built-in kitchens. All these elements were opportunities to use slashes and dashes of colour to highlight and emphasize the function of the pieces.

Freestanding furniture, too, was changing; the development of completely new materials and techniques such as moulded plastic and fibreglass meant that new designs of chairs, for example, were also being produced in vibrant, bright colours and sinuous, exciting shapes. This is why so many designs from the 1950s and 1960s, with their immediately recognizable and uncompromising shapes, are so popular today in contemporary interiors, adding, as they do, both a colourful element to a modern room and also an interesting and individual link to the past.

CASE STUDY

SPIRIT OF LE CORBUSIER

A vivacity and a 1950s ambience pervade this apartment in the Malmousque quartier in Marseille, a home inspired by the works of the great Swiss-born French architect Le Corbusier.

When they first arrived in Marseille – the *cité phocéenne*, as it is sometimes called, after its founders in 600BC – the Parisian owners of this apartment explored from one end of the city to the other, trying to really get to know every neighbourhood – and there are many of them. They loved the air, the clear light, the coastline and, of course, the bantering jokes of this city of the mistral, the strong northwesterly wind that whistles through on a regular basis.

As they climbied the steps of this small, rather anodyne 1950s building, the first thing they noticed was the view, with – directly opposite – the Frioul islands and the Château d'If, looking as if they were but a bat's squeak away. They asked a local firm of architects, ADR, led by Henry Roussel and Eric Steiner, if they could make something of the 65m² (699 square feet) pied-à-terre. It was decided to revamp what was basically a characterless concrete box using a colour palette of about twelve strong colours, furniture and objects from the 1950s and referencing Le Corbusier in everything – from the use of colour to the choice of pieces and, of course, the layout and arrangement of the space.

Above The bustling city of Marseille, where Le Corbusier implemented many of his innovative ideas in architecture and design.
Right The open kitchen of the apartment with a countertop in techno quartz. The colours of the made-to-measure storage units are a bright, citrus mix. The trio of pendant lights are pressed glass and steel.
Far right In the living room, a no.71 armchair by Eero Saarinen from 1951 and a low, vintage, Danish table in teak. An oak sideboard/storage unit from the 1950s boasts sliding doors in lime-yellow, and the striking rug picks up all the colours used in the apartment, and more besides.

Opposite Close to the entrance hall and leading out from the sitting space is the dining area, organized around a 1960s green-glazed Kéramos Sèvres ceramic dish on the table. On the sideboard, below the striking sunray mirror, is a black metal lamp from 1955.
Left The small different rooms of the small apartment segue seamlessly into each other through the clever use of sliding doors, which maximize the space and make circulation simple.
Below A bedroom is painted in raspberry-pink, its design demonstrating ingenuity in the wall storage with belongings hidden behind sliding doors and camouflaged in drawers beneath the bed. A striking ceiling lamp in lacquered aluminium dates from the 1950s.

An early design decision, and one which made sense in this small space, was to have only sliding doors, to make circulation easy and add space. The walls were coloured sea-blue. And yellow. And orange. Yet more blocks of clear, bright colour were added in the walls of display alcoves and the pieces of furniture. The windows were hung with discreet blinds (shades) rather than curtains, the better to enjoy the bright daylight and to see the sea. The floor was laid with wide strips of Danish teak, which also serves as an acoustic barrier. Air-conditioning was discreetly incorporated into the fabric of the apartment – in other words, all the basic elements were made to be as self-effacing and as practical as possible, to allow the objects and furniture from the 1950s that the couple have collected to take centre stage.

The architects designed, and made to measure, the storage units, and all, including those in the kitchen, the bathroom and master bedroom, were planned down to the last, fine, detail. In the second bedroom, intended for children, grandchildren or passing guests, what appears a storage unit along one wall becomes, in one easy movement, a pair of beds, one above the other – *à la couchette*.

Thought about and planned to the last detail, this apartment has turned out to be, amid the colours of the sun, an easy and pleasant place to live.

CASE STUDY

FIFTIES PRESERVED

The villa La Rafale was designed by Pierre Marmouget between 1957 and 1959, as one of the projects marking the renewal of the city of Royan, in France, which had been so heavily bombed at the end of the Second World War.

This is a house full of history. When the city of Royan was to be rebuilt after the war, it was decided not to reproduce the original architecture but to rebuild in the modernist style. Among the young architects commissioned to design houses was Pierre Marmouget, who designed the villa La Rafale seen here – a house that is sometimes now known, for obvious reasons, as The Boomerang.

The owners of La Rafale wanted to go into the future with an avant-garde design; they had been inspired by the work of the Brazilian architect Oscar Niemeyer, and after seeing

Opposite, above A curved walkway stretches sinuously around the avant-garde design of this 1950s house, sometimes known as 'The Boomerang'.
Opposite, below Trees shade and partly hide the façade of the villa. The swimming pool is surrounded by a specially designed barrier as well as rounded sunbeds in bright colours.
This page The sitting room and dining room, flooded with natural light and filled with furniture that was custom-designed for the villa when it was originally built.

another villa that Marmouget had designed, gave him carte blanche to create a holiday house for them in a modernist style. It was an ambitious design, set on piles and in the curved form of a boomerang. It used many new techniques and materials, incorporated glass walls into the façade, light-reflecting tiles on the roof and an open honeycomb wall inside that diffused light throughout the interior.

For privacy, Marmouget introduced yellow-and-blue sliding shutter doors. It is a perfectly thought-out scheme that even has a touch of eccentric fantasy, such as the permanent ladder that drops directly from the raised verandah above, down into the swimming pool below.

It is a vacation house designed to receive many guests. The owners, who also owned a vineyard, Moulin-Haut-Laroque, in Bordeaux, often invited other wine professionals to come to their home and the reception rooms were designed with that in mind. Marmouget designed a long dining table and chairs as well, with, close to hand, a curved, cushioned bench leading to an inviting bar, complete with stools. In the sitting area, armchairs and small tables were arranged in small convivial groups.

In the 1990s Thomas Hervé, great-nephew of the first owners, realized that he should conserve this amazing piece of 1950s modernist design and began to look into archives and old photographs to see how the house had looked when it was first built. With the help of photograph albums and old reels of Super 8 home movies, he built up a picture of where every piece of furniture and object had originally stood. Much of the furniture had been made to measure by Marmouget to combine both function and comfort, and Hervé was keen to re-create the original setting, with everything in its original place. He wanted the villa to keep the purity of its origins. 'After all,' he says, 'I have a duty of memory.'

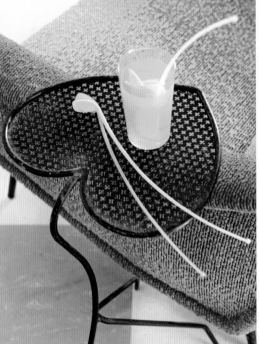

Opposite, above Curves and more curves in the form of a honeycomb wall that winds its way around the upper floor, diffusing light through the building.
Opposite, below left As modern-looking today as when it was built, a fiery red outdoor fireplace, set into the wall by the pool, with an assymetrical low table that curves around a post.
Opposite, below centre Originally designed as convivial areas where guests could pass the time, the many comfortable nooks and crannies were designed for relaxation.
Opposite, below right and below The lines and colours, materials as well as the furniture and decoration at Marmouget look as strikingly modern today as they did in the 1950s.
Right The bench seats and stools of the bar area, like the armchairs in the games room, were specifically designed for meetings, receptions and the tastings that the original owners would have with their fellow vignerons. In this room, another innovative design is the freestanding fireplace, the chimney clad in beaten copper.

CASE STUDY GRAPHIC DESIGN

Traditional Provence is hot and sunny, a rocky landscape splashed with light, and memories of Marcel Pagnol's evocative book La Gloire de Mon Père, *but, here, hidden in the Alpilles, is a modernist surprise.*

Gérard Faivre is a well-known interior designer who works across Europe. He sees himself not just as a decorator, nor an architect, nor landscape designer – just simply a bit of everything all at the same time. His secret is that he dares to design without inhibitions, to stretch the bounds of the traditional, adding new twists of originality and surprise. So it is with this old farmhouse in Provence, where he has cleverly combined the classical with the contemporary.

Above *This house in the Alpilles of southern France is a restored traditional farmhouse, now in use as a holiday guesthouse. In its new guise it combines country architecture with vintage and modernist design.*
Left *Entirely rearranged and restructured, the reception rooms, dining room and office now all combine a melange of contemporary and vintage design. The walls are papered in a Sanderson re-edition of a 1950s design, and the ceiling has been lined with stripped cane. The sofas and chairs are by Cappellini.*
Right *In the library/office, beyond the main reception room, a pair of vintage Utah chairs in front of a tear-drop table on which is displayed some of Gérard Faivre's collection of modernist ceramics.*

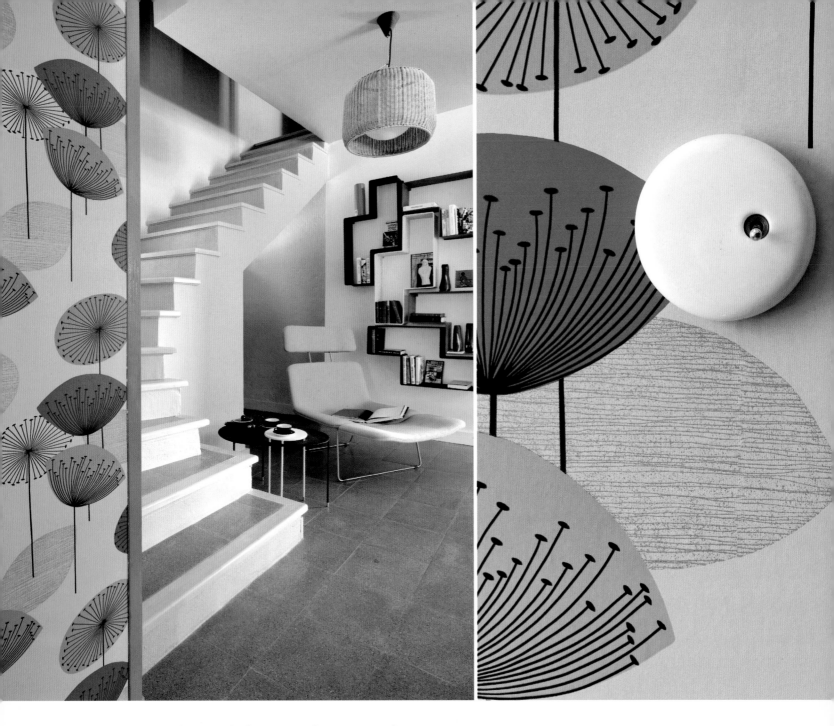

The garden, for example, features, as do so many gardens in this region, box, lavender and an olive grove, but here the box and lavender are grown out of brightly coloured lacquered metal tubs in the colours of Provence – sky, sun and earth – and the grass between the geometric design is bright green and synthetic.

The owner of this house wanted something unique, a house that did not conform to the norm. Perfect for Mr Faivre, who likes to create every aspect of every object from A to Z and beginning to end, as if every house was going to belong to him. Sometimes he works from scratch, even down to selecting the land, but on this project it was a question of restoring a *mas* that the owner wished to use as a bed-and-breakfast holiday location, which

Above left At the base of the open staircase leading to the bedrooms is a geometric open wall unit for storing books and objects. The table below is by Gubi, and the chaise longue is Spring by Erwan Bourollec, for Cappellini.
Above right These circular, porcelain, electric light switches are mood-perfect both for the wallpaper design and the style of the whole house.
Opposite Opening onto the terrace outside, the red bedroom has one wall with a strong wallpaper of stylized seed heads, a re-edition by Sanderson. The kelim-covered chair picks out the right colours and adds another element of pattern, and the knotted standard lamp is topped with a suitably retro fringed shade.

Below In another bedroom, a suitably futuristic arrangement of elliptical book-holders are ranged in different sizes and shapes along the wall.

he wanted designed with wit and a lightness of touch. It was a major project: walls had to be opened up, rooms created, everything designed to welcome guests. The success of the project is the way that the contemporary and retro-style furniture and furnishings work so well with the traditional lines of the *mas* – the curved doors and deep-set windows, as well as ceiling beams, often infilled with panels of rushes or hemp. The entrance hall, for example, has a specially designed wrought-iron screen in 1950s style that breaks up the space, on a modern terrazzo floor, which runs through the house. Against walls

papered with reeditions of 1950s designs, the reception and dining rooms are furnished in a style that is partly contemporary and partly harking back to the mid-twentieth century, as are the bedrooms, each of which is individually and brightly decorated, and many of them leading directly out onto the terrace. There is a wooden-decked, tree-hidden outdoor swimming pool – *bien sûr*, this is Provence, after all. But there is also, less usual, a new inside pool complete with sauna and hammam. And around the side of the house, a balmy summer evening's special: an outdoor cinema, the icing on the cake!

Below left *The dressing room of the master bedroom was designed by Gérard Faivre with custom-built wardrobe storage and a comfortable vintage armchair.*
Below right *The master bedroom is a study in neutral cool with a quiet patterned wallpaper, a bed by Paola Navone, a low table and a flying-saucer-like floor lamp.*

CASE STUDY DECORATOR'S DEN

To restore both life and style to the home of the 1950s decorator Jacques Dumond was the fascinating challenge taken up by the new owners of this apartment.

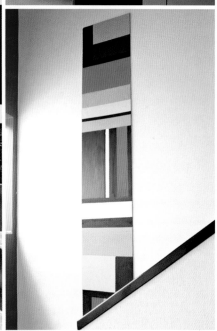

The 16th arrondisement of Paris is home to a concentration of the work of the architect Jean Ginsberg, a disciple of Robert Mallet-Stevens, Le Corbusier and Lurçat. On the upper floor of one of these buildings, the architect and decorator Jacques Dumond took up residence in the 1950s. Dumond was an architect, decorator and furniture designer of the period – a modernist from the group led by Adolf Loos and Mies van der Rohe, who, having studied cabinet-making at L'Ecole Boulle, conceived the idea of designing entire architectural ensembles rather than isolated pieces of furniture. Unsurprisingly, he designed his own apartment to be a discerning combination of discipline and luxury.

The new owners of the apartment, who bought it from Dumond's son, had hitherto not known of the designer, but soon discovered the man and his work, and decided they wanted to re-create the style of Dumond and his period in the design and decoration of the apartment. They researched the history of the area and the decorative style

Above, left In the courtyard of the apartment building is a geometric fresco by the Cuban artist Wilfredo Arçay, who lived in Paris from the 1940s.
Above, top The communal block of letter boxes on the ground floor, set in a wall of bright blue.
Above A fresco on the staircase wall, which was painted in 1960, has been restored under the aegis of L'Atelier du Temps Passé.
Opposite In the main living room are a pair of the famous Lounge Chairs by Charles and Ray Eames on a geometric rug of the same period. The futuristic tripod floor light is by Boris Lacroix.

of the period – the pared-down lines, the type of materials used that Dumond combined with strong colours and pattern in pictures, hangings and furniture.

Then they were introduced to Frank Schmidt. This was a fortunate meeting, for Schmidt, an interior decorator and antique dealer, knew exactly how to furnish and equip the apartment in the right period. So, with the consent of the owners, he put together pieces with unusual and surprising connections. Around Eero Saarinen's famous Tulip table, for example, he combined not the matching chairs but contrasting styles, one by Robin Day, the British designer of the same period, which the couple added to with their own design themes – for him Chomo sculptures, for her a collection of vintage Barbie dolls.

A serendipitous moment occurred when Schmidt tracked down a copy of *La Maison Française* dated May 1960 – an issue that featured this very apartment; from the feature, he was able to see what had disappeared from the space and could be replaced, and what still remained from the original scheme. Although many of the innovative, design features no longer existed, others had escaped the hand of renovation, including, wonderfully, a pull-out shelf that revealed an illuminated bar with hidden bottles of aperitifs; the only things that were missing from the unit were the original gramophone, speaker and collection of LPs. It's fair to say that Jacques Dumond's heritage inspired a habitat turned squarely towards the future.

Above In the dining area of the open-plan apartment, a Tulip table by Eero Saarinen, with a wall – and most of the apartment – dominated by a wall hanging by Alexander Calder.
Left The original storage units in Formica were designed by Jaques Dumond and now restored. On a low table is part of a collection of period ceramics – a sculpture by the twentieth-century artist Chomo; on a plinth against the wall is a piece by the post-war ceramic artist Michel Lucotte.
Opposite The living room seen from the far side, with a chimneypiece in steel and stone that dominates its surroundings, and a bright-coloured chair by Bertoia. The flow through the apartment is facilitated by the simple polished wooden flooring and the neutral colours used on the walls and woodwork.

Eclectic

Eclectic retro – or bonkers chic, as it is sometimes affectionately termed – could perhaps be described as that evanescent, will-o'-the-wisp style that, when put together by masters of the genre, looks wonderful, intriguing, fascinating and individual, but when put together by an amateur of the look becomes simply a collection or group of disparate objects and furniture – a discombobulating, jangling jumble.

In an eclectic interior or home, it is easy to say that anything goes, but it is also important not to take such an injunction too literally. Anything goes, as long as it goes. It's like the difference between a soup where everything in the refrigerator is thrown into the pot, and one where one or two ingredients are carefully blended; the intention might be the same but the outcome is entirely different.

Right *A busy room, packed with things to delight and amuse the eye. The back wall is filled with a single bookcase designed by Hans Wettstein. In front of it stands a black leather chaise longue by Le Corbusier, separated by a metal side table from an Empire daybed, upholstered in dark velvet. In one corner, an apple-green velvet chair by Jean Nouvel, and hanging from above, a film floodlight, recycled into a ceiling lamp.*
Below *The fireplace, inspired by the fanciful monsters of the Bomarzo gardens near Rome, is set into a black-and-white chequerboard chimney piece, almost heraldic in spirit. Other elements include a black wing chair by Carlo Mollino and, to one side, an onrate folding screen decorated by Edward Burne-Jones.*

Below In a Moroccan house of colourful charm and contrast, an African armchair embroidered with beans stands next to a low Danish sideboard dating from the 1950s.

Opposite In a restored house in Tunis, a room of contrast. Ornate tiled walls and two low-hung, beautiful antique chandeliers set off a table made of white-painted planks on metal trestle legs, where a resin crow waits for crumbs. The chairs too are in contrast – simple of shape and inspired by the 1950s. Behind the table, a picture, L'Elu by Ibrahim Mattous.

Some eclectic retro schemes are born from the nomadic instinct. The traveller – either in reality or in dreams – brings his spoils together under one roof, where they act as memories or daydreams of a life of adventure.

And then there are those interiors that are the result of a collector's fancy – usually a collector happier in flea markets than grand antique salerooms, in places where he – or she – picks up something quirky, something spirited, something damaged, but all with a charm and a certain *je ne sais quoi* that he finds he cannot live without.

Then there are those who love old things, but not one sort of old thing, nor one period, nor style – they love it all and want to live with it, convention notwithstanding, and see no problem in bringing them all together, centuries and styles happily mixed up in one giant pot-pourri.

Wherever the starting point, these interiors are always comfortable – well, maybe not in the conventional sense; the chairs might sometimes need the help of an extra seat cushion, the bed an added mattress – but they are pleasing because the owner is comfortable with them and wishes those who come to visit to share the pleasure that he derives from each object.

From this it is easy to see that eclectic style is immeasurably idiosyncratic, and is very much an expression of the owner's personality, who has, above all, a good eye for what will work with what and where. This is not to say that lesser mortals cannot achieve such effects. The important thing to remember is that for all the apparent devil-may-care placing and arranging of these rooms, they all actually conform to the basic rules of good interior design and decoration – particularly those most important rules of proportion, scale and balance. It is these qualities that make a room appealing and make one feel at home, even if it is not styled as one's home is.

In all the rooms featured here for example, the objects and furniture themselves may be unusual or unconventional and teamed with others equally so, but they have all been placed in groups that have a certain, if unconventional, symmetry – the massive open jaws of the metal fireplace in the picture on page 90 is balanced by the black-and-white chequerboard of the chimney piece behind it; each cancels the other out. What is hung on the walls – not always pictures – is used again to balance what stands on the floor, grouped in sometimes unconventional but always complementary ways. Every room is thought about and, you may be sure, changed and changed again until, in the owner's eye, it is absolutely perfect.

Below The large sitting room – a salon de repos – was painted a warm red by Giorgio Silvagni. Rugs cover the traditionally set cobblestone floor. Pieces from the eighteenth century are mixed with objets, lights, furniture and ceramics from the twentieth century, much of it found in the flea markets of Villeneuve-lès-Avignon.

Opposite In one corner, a collection of ceramics from the Vallauris pottery, lit by a lamp sporting a basket-weave shade.

CASE STUDY CENTURIES OF STYLE

In the countryside near Avignon, Irene Silvagni's old bastide is furnished with a mixture of styles as personal as they are surprising.

Walking into Irene Silvagni's old Provençal *bastide* feels a bit like arriving at the house of an old friend. Whether that is to do with the proportions of the rooms, the instinctive elegance of the owner, or the warmth of the welcome is a difficult question – possibly a bit of all of those things. Generosity here is a habit, an act of faith in life and in other people.

Irene and her late husband Giorgio bought the house after seeing it advertised as a 'Ruin for Sale'. Ruin it might have been, half-hidden by brambles, but a charming one, dating from the seventeenth century, with rooms of noble proportions, beams and arches and centuries-old floors, some of them cobbled.

Each as creative as each other – Irene, once editor of French *Vogue* and then consultant to Yohji Yamamoto, Giorgio, film producer and artist – they slowly and carefully worked their way through the once noble rooms. While Irene scoured the flea markets and antique shops in the area, Giorgio painted the walls with shimmering, glistening washes of colour – reds, greens and blues – sometimes roughly

applied, sometimes patinated and polished, or presented as fat stripes of colour. These walls are more than a background; they are an integral part of the theatre that is this house. Set within this rush of colour, the house is filled with a collection that can truly be called eclectic – old furniture from the seventeenth century matched with pieces from the 1960s – where the decorative and the industrial peacefully cohabit. There are objects and ceramics (particularly pottery from Vallauris), eighteenth-century paintings, fashion photos and portraits. There are also textiles – old and new – wherever you look and used in combination with everything else; hung on walls, made into cushions and draped over sofas, chairs and tables. 'It was all a question of where to put everything,' Irene explains, 'but Giorgio had the innate sense of a director, a real talent for creating compositions and producing combinations of objects that were foreign to one another but resonated with each other.'

In a house like this, where rooms flow into each other and function is fluid, there will always be an adjustment to be made here, an arrangement to be changed there. Irene is now turning her attention to one of the barns. And why not? This is the sort of house and the sort of project that, happily, will never be completely finished.

Above The small Turkish room is filled with textiles, kelims and pieces of family furniture, with walls that have been washed in colour and patinated.
Right A collector to her soul, Irene has filled and covered every surface with objets trouvés. Here, on a table next to the bed, is a small and eclectic selection.
Far right In a bedroom where the original stone floor has been retained in all its imperfect glory, and where old and new pieces of furniture live happily together, Giorgio painted the walls a pale leaf-green with a delicate fresco of olive branches that winds round the room.
Opposite A reading room was brought into being by Giorgio with the installation of a basic mobile bookshelf and an old set of simple shelving. The colours of the room are more neutral in tone than elsewhere in the house, a combination of ochre and cream. The furniture is a combination of styles, including a pair of Mies van der Rohe leather Barcelona chairs and a cane and metal chair.

CASE STUDY GLAMPING BRITISH STYLE

As so often, it was happy childhood holidays that were the germ of Anna Bingham and partner Dan Mullaly's love affair with caravans, but it wasn't until Dan's parents decided to sell their old Mercedes camper van that Dan and Anna realized that, for both of them, this was a love affair that was not going to die.

Anna is a designer, who in an earlier life launched and designed a lingerie line; Dan is a tour manager for bands. In 2007 Anna and Dan had just moved back to Cornwall, from where they both hailed, and decided that they wanted to create an unusual – unique even – version of a camping site. In order to profit from the 'glamping' craze, they opened a campsite that, rather than using tents as accommodation, would encompass their love of vintage caravans, camping vans and old buses and offer a group of the above as overnight havens. As with all obsessions, they became infatuated with their new project, and started to search for treasures on wheels – old school buses, gypsy caravans, traditional trailers – in brief, models that were essentially British, and difficult to track down. Their first buys were a plump,

pink, little Sterling two-bed caravan, circa 1958, which they christened Valerie, and, in contrast, a flashy showman's caravan from the 1970s that used to be pulled behind a fairground waltzer. These were soon joined by an iconic American Silver Bullet and one of the earliest of trailer caravans, the Carlight. The camping site – Love Lane Caravans – was up and running – or rather not running, but safely grounded in the field that Anna and Dan had rented.

The interiors of the vehicles differed enormously; the showman's caravan was an exemplar of showman chic – showmen like their formica, chrome and stainless steel, with touches of gilding and bevelled glass. Kitsch perhaps but glamorous kitsch. Others, like the old school bus, were more rudimentary and not designed for eating and sleeping, and so had to be adapted to camping holidays.

So far, so slightly unusual, but what gave Love Lane Caravans their even more unusual edge is the way that Dan, with a team of local specialist craftsmen, renovated these snail houses into eccentric and charming homes from home, and Anna furnished and embellished them. Anna's design preference – well, her love, really – is for vintage everything: flower-patterned china, old-fashioned eiderdowns, bright-patterned jugs. Buying from the usual vintage treasure-troves – vintage shops, car-boot sales, local markets – she has amassed a cache of individual pieces that she carefully places in the caravans.

Opposite, above Dating from the late 1950s, this was once a rural bus, the Tiger Cub made by Leyland. Now retired from the country lanes, it has been transformed by Anna and the group of craftsmen that she uses into one of several quirky homes-from-home.

Opposite, below Many of the original interior fittings have been retained, including some of the original bench seats, which have been re-upholstered and some re-positioned to make an eating area, which Anna has now furnished with pieces from her collection of vintage, floral china.

Right At the back of the bus is a romantic canopied bed.

This page and opposite In the years between 1950 and 1970, Vickers, the caravan makers, produced a range of caravans specifically for Romany travellers. Ornate and individual, they were finished to the nth, and most expensive, degree with exteriors bristling with chrome, and the interiors finished with polished oak, stainless steel, cut and etched mirrored glass and acres of Formica. The upholstery was deeply buttoned and trimmed, and fitted Axminster carpet was provided for the flooring. Kitsch these carvans were, but glorious too. This model dates from the end of the 1960s, and Anna and Dan have not altered the interior, merely restoring when necessary and adding glass and ceramics in the same travellers' style.

CASE STUDY INTERNATIONAL ECCENTRICITY

Two steps away from the City of London, in the heart of the fashionable quarter in East London, a Frenchman, a Malaysian and a Swede have created 'Les Trois Garçons'. A little empire in the heart of Shoreditch, where France meets England, this small world consists of a restaurant, bar and a shop. On the first floor is their apartment.

Left *Above an antique Louis XV bench seat hangs a nineteenth-century painting of King Karl Johan of Sweden. Either side of the portrait is a pair of mirrors that once belonged to the royal family of Savoy.*

Above and opposite *The main reception room of Les Trois Garçons is an exercise in opulence, with a wealth of objects from all periods and in all styles arranged together, including a pair of painted Louis XVI chairs with the Trois Garçons monogram embroidered on each one. The disparate grouping includes a Swedish Empire period chandelier, a nineteenth-century Royal Doulton jardinière and a nineteenth-century French mirror. It all works well because each piece, from a Roman head to a low white contemporary table, is of equal weight and authority.*

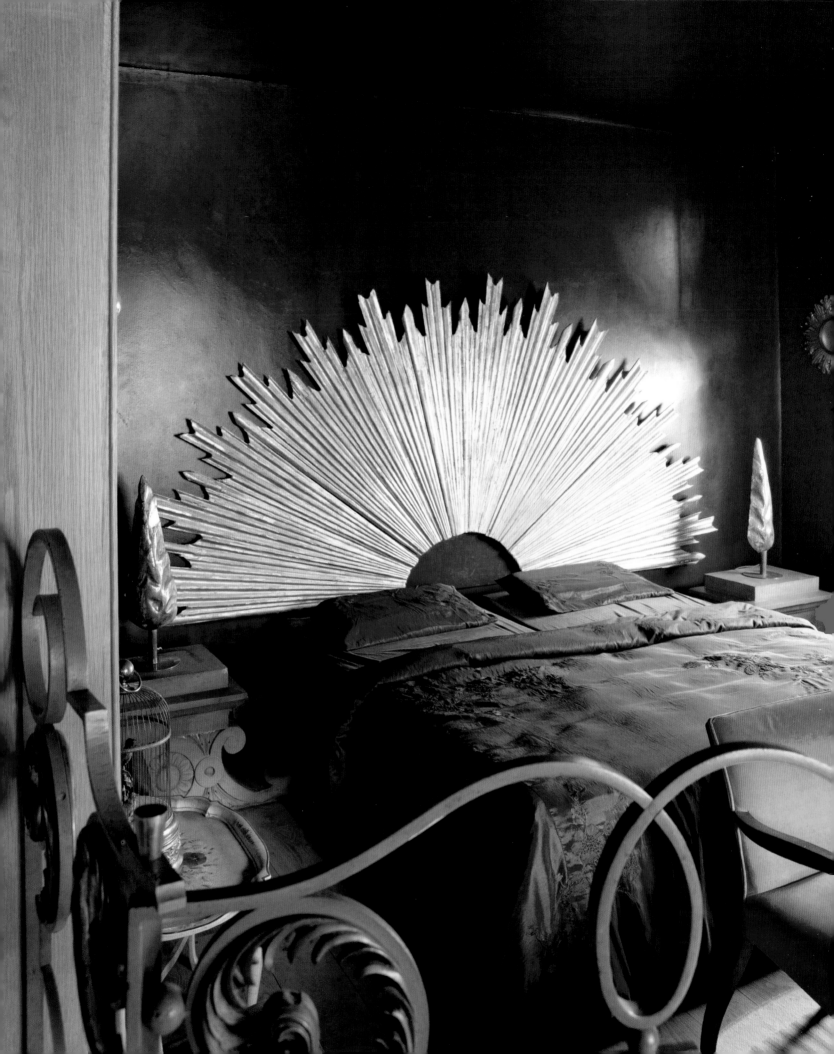

Opposite and right *The master bedroom – known as la chambre solaire – is a celebration of light and dark. Against a wall of deepest blue, the walls are punctuated by a collection of mirrors framed in gilded wood, and smaller sunbursts framing clocks and portraits. The largest sunburst of all, an oversized gilded piece dating from the seventeenth century, is employed as a striking bedhead. The piece comes originally from an Italian church. There is a contrast of material as well as periods: wrought iron, polished wood and mirrored glass cupboards.*

Michel, Hassan and Stefan came to London to study and perfect their English. But that was not all that happened. They liked London – liked it so much that they decided to make their base there and take up antique dealing and interior decorating. They looked around and, in 1996 they came across an old Victorian pub in the East End of London, round the corner from the City and also Brick Lane. After all, if you're going to immerse yourself in London life, what could be more to the point than a pub in Shoreditch? They took it on, creating an apartment on the first floor of the building and, a few years later,

made the ground floor into a restaurant, named 'Les Trois Garçons', naturally. The restaurant and apartment are both decorated in the same style, which is very original. Refined by their antique dealing and their interior decorating, the look definitely leans towards the eccentric: taxidermy, of course, mixed with nineteenth-century pieces, 1970s furniture and everything in between. They cite the twentieth-century American interior decorator Tony Duquette, famous for claiming that 'More is More' and the equally famous Dorothy Draper – both of them flamboyant, both original, both exponents of modern baroque – as their inspirations.

'London offers us an unbelievable creative freedom, a place where anything and everything is possible,' says Michel, and certainly in the decorative juxtapositions, both in the apartment and in the restaurant – which is treated decoratively as an extension of the living quarters – all is fair game. Literally, in one case – as the crowned head of the wall-hung stuffed giraffe's head on the restaurant wall attests. Upstairs, in the corridor that leads to the bedrooms, a line of antique handbags is hung along a wall interspersed with floating vintage dresses, demonstrating the beauty of function.

They understand the strength of putting together simple or apparently ordinary objects: Fulham Pottery white-glazed ceramic vases designed by and made for the 1950s florist and cook Constance Spry, are grouped close together to create a striking composition. Even the Trois Garçons' shoes – from a wide selection of trainers to polished leathers – are stored and displayed in made-to-measure glass-fronted oak cabinets.

On the furniture front, anything and everything goes; periods and styles are combined seemingly with abandon – except that such apparent abandon is actually very carefully considered. It is impossible to put together sofas and armchairs from almost every decade of the twentieth century alongside nineteenth-century French mirrors, Bohemian coloured-glass chandeliers and, even in a bedroom, a seventeenth-century sunburst from an Italian church, used as a striking bedhead, without complete confidence. Confidence and a great deal of natural style – and that these Trois Garçons have in spades.

Opposite, left *Along the corridor that leads to the bedrooms is a collection of vintage frocks and bags that, instead of being left hidden from view in a cupboard, are displayed on the walls as fashion ornamentation.*

Opposite, right *In the small and cosy sitting room, under the artwork, Rebis, by Matthew Stradling, and on a mirrored console table, is a collection of vases from the Fulham Pottery, made for the famous florist Constance Spry. The chairs are by Verner Panton.*

Right *The dressing room that leads off the master bedroom was designed by the Trois Garçons. Cabinets in light oak and with glass-fronted doors show racks of shoes and trainers in an efficient way. In front is a pair of 1950s armchairs upholstered in Italian velvet. The ceiling light is English – a brass flambeau style dating from the nineteenth century.*

CASE STUDY CABINET OF CURIOSITIES

From the fashion house of Christian Lacroix comes a collection of individual and original furnishings, seen at their sparkling best in the Parisian apartment of Lacroix's creative director, Sacha Walckhoff.

Exotic and baroque, the Parisian apartment of Sacha Walckhoff is a reflection of the world of Christian Lacroix. Having worked closely with the couturier for seventeen years, Sacha has now taken over as creative director of the fashion house, and is taking it into other areas, including home décor and decoration.

A meeting with Tricia Guild, founder of Designers Guild, has led to the creation, under Sacha Walckhoff's guiding hand, of a line of furnishings destined for decoration. The collection, edited and distributed by Designers Guild, includes such exotica as fur rugs, cut velvet, textile panels and cushions, cushions everywhere.

In Sacha's apartment, many of the elements of this new Lacroix project are combined with his own eccentric and unusual objects, everything arranged and placed with care and thought. A traveller and lover of travel, he lives in what can only be described as a contemporary cabinet of curiosities, which reflects the wide range of his tastes and influences.

This page The living room, a riot of pattern and colour, period and style. By the fireplace, an armchair signed by Raphaël and a fireside stool from the 1960s by Pierre Paulin. Nesting tables from the 1950s by Mategot and a coffee table by Capron, on which is a bird vase by Picasso. The sofa and cushions are striped in grey with, in the background, a deep chair covered in a Christian Lacroix fabric.
Opposite On a zebra-striped rug, Riviera, an antique wooden stool with turned, gilded legs, covered with a striped silk fabric, Sol y Sombra, from Christian Lacroix.

He is a collector of ceramics, a lover of contemporary design and a devotee of furniture from the 1950s. To be found throughout the apartment are such assorted fineries as vases by Picasso and Hella Jongerius, stools by modernist architect and designer Charlotte Perriand, a pedestal table from Garouste and Bonnetti and drawings by Jean Cocteau. A veritable roll call of twentieth-century masters, but everything edited with discipline and taste, as might be expected.

It is also unusual: in the hallway an oversized half-torso of a zebra appears to canter out of the wall. In the sitting room, the windows are shaded with strips of perforated openwork and a commanding statue of a black torch bearer, liberally hung with strings of bright beads, faces a sofa covered in a Lacroix fabric of broad black and white stripes with animal print cushions, set on a zebra print rug; throughout the apartment a love of animal prints is not just evident but all-pervading.

Opposite, top left *In the study, on either side of the paned mirror, is a pair of masks by Garouste and Bonnetti from the 1980s. The two simple 1960s stools at one side of the mirror are by Florence Knoll. The red velvet-covered armchair is from Designers Guild. The room is held together by the striking zebra-print rug.*

Opposite, top right *In the foreground, 'Nègre à la torchère', a prop from the film* The Count of Monte Cristo. *On the wall, a mosaic made up of a collection of photos, prints, and drawings.*

Opposite, below *In the distance, the salon, as seen through two tall, slightly precarious columns of books, which in shape and form are as decorative as they are practical.*

Right *The kitchen is as surprising as the rest of the apartment, with the large, ornate and decorative Syrian cabinet here used as a commodious storage cupboard. The chairs around the table are from Bertoia and Tolix, and the cushions are by Christian Lacroix for Designers Guild.*

This page In the bedroom, a striking screen in cowhide and a pair of bedside tables designed by Jacques Adnet in the 1940s, metal lamps by Boris Lacroix and a bed cover made from Paseo Doble, a Lacroix design for Designers Guild.

There was a dining room in the apartment, but no more; Sacha has done away with it, feeling it served no useful purpose, and has changed the space into a study, which is, as you might expect, crammed with columns of books – on art, fashion, design, literature, photography and history.

The more you gaze into the depths of the apartment, the more you realize the strong sense of taste and style that lie behind what seems at first glance to be simply an interesting mélange of well-loved, mismatched colours and objects. But the groupings – of ceramics on open shelves, of pictures and photographs hung on a wall, of the careful placing of disparate pieces of furniture around the fireplace – could only have been conceived by someone with a strong sense of style and artistic confidence. And as Sacha himself says, 'My apartment is not a showroom where designs and new lines are displayed, it is an exact reflection of my innermost personality.'

Above *On the left, looking back from the drawing room to the bedroom, towards a large, wall-hung photograph by Daniel Firman. On the right, the reverse view from the bedroom, looking into the drawing room, is a stool by Tapio Wirkala and a vibrant pair of illustrations by Antonio.*
Right *Within the luxurious excess of the apartment there is still a rigorous sense of order, with a place for everything and storage fitted in every corner.*

DETAILS THAT COUNT

Archetypal retro signatures

ALTHOUGH THE TERM RETRO can mean many things to many people, as far as the details are concerned – the furniture, the textiles, the accessories – there are some key pieces and shapes that everyone now recognizes as being representative of that whole period. Inevitably, of course, it is the chair that, for many, defines retro design, which is unsurprising since many early twentieth-century chairs, by designers such as Walter Gropius and Mies van der Rohe, are now rightly recognized as being exemplars of twentieth-century design. In their time, they were considered both original and innovative (albeit by a relatively small group of enthusiasts) and we can appreciate these qualities today, as well as valuing the more prosaic but necessary attributes of beauty and comfort.

But retro design was not of course limited to major pieces of furniture; the interest in using new materials and new technology manifested itself in all aspects of interior design and decoration, from furnishing fabrics to ceramics and glass. There was a curiosity and a desire to create something new, and many of the quirkier pieces that can be found today – particularly the more decorative pieces such as the delightful, quintessentially retro sunray mirrors – are as redolent of their time as anything designed by an old master.

There is a romance now attached to many of these pieces and, indeed, to the period itself, and if you find yourself drawn to this era then a good entry point might be to incorporate one or more of these smaller pieces – the accents, so to speak – into your current look. Although when seen in isolation, some of these designs – a lamp, a mirror, a piece of ceramic or glass – might look almost too individual, when added to the mix of what you already have, there is no doubt that any one will lift and lighten the spirits of a room.

Left A typically retro grouping of objects – a sun mirror with cane rays and a collection of ceramics by Capron, all illuminated by a Sputnik lamp.

Opposite Against a bright red wall, a 1950s chair customized in geometric/ abstract style by the designer Cécile Chicot; a glass-topped table is the base for an antique wooden statuette.

Furnishings

Retro style is a broad church, a place where inventiveness and originality of design are always present. The sleek lines, the simple shapes, are powerful arguments for including a retro piece in a contemporary room. It hasn't always been the case that good design has also been both comfortable and functional – this was an unusual period on many levels. There is a grace and fluidity and also a flexibility in twentieth-century furniture and furnishings, so it is perhaps no surprise that the different elements of the style, from the lighting to the furnishing fabrics, the tables and the chairs, all work so well together, as well as with pieces from other periods. But if you are testing the retro water, so to speak, it might be more fruitful to look first at one area of design rather than plunge into every aspect of the style. Perhaps you have an affinity for textiles or a passion for chairs. By concentrating on a single theme, both your knowledge and your 'eye' – that indefinable recognition of a key piece – will get the very best out of what is there.

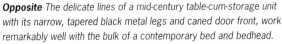

Opposite The delicate lines of a mid-century table-cum-storage unit with its narrow, tapered black metal legs and caned door front, work remarkably well with the bulk of a contemporary bed and bedhead.

Above left Positioned near a bedroom window, an undulating cane chair, vintage in origin, Asian in feel.
Above right Vintage shapes from the 1950s – the patinated chest of drawers and the upholstered chair – are linked by a soft turquoise colour on chair, glass and picture frames.

SEATING

The chair is so much a part of our daily lives that we sometimes barely notice it, even when we are sitting on it. Depicted from ancient times in paintings and ceramics in all its variety and charm, its history is, in many ways, both the history of domestic life and that of changing social patterns and fashions. It is also the story of furniture design. Some of the earliest chairs – the beautiful Greek klismos with its curve of leg and back, for example, and the X-framed stool seen in both Egyptian and Greek illustrations – are still influencing chair design today. Although for other than the ruling classes, where a chair – often in the form of a throne – denoted power and rank, such sophisticated forms of seating were not normally seen in western society until many centuries had passed and stools and benches were, for the common man, the usual and everyday form of seating for hundreds of years.

These early, basic forms of seating had very little to do with comfort or fashion and everything to do with practicality; the three- or four-legged wooden stool, for example, was hardly a thing of comfort but it served its purpose and knew its place, as indeed, relatively speaking, did a more luxurious version, an X-framed stool, known as a *tabouret*, which

Above left *A curvy, buttoned leather chair designed by George Mulhauser in the 1950s at home in a nineteenth-century, classically proportioned room.*
Far left *Leather has always been a traditional choice for buttoned-back sofas, and this classic early twentieth-century Chesterfield sofa is perfectly at home in a more retro-style room*
Left *Upstairs in a house in Provence, a Barcelona chair designed by Mies van der Rohe is perfectly at home against a soft washed mint colour wall and on an old tiled floor.*
Opposite *A classic leather buttoned Eames chair with its ottoman. In design contrast, next to the French window, is a desk and matching chair designed in the 1960s by Marc Berthier.*

was in use in grand households and European courts. The sixteenth-century diarist, the Duc de Saint-Simon, famously documented the jostling rivalry among the nobles at the court of Louis XIV, where protocol dictated that only those of high rank, rather than standing with the crowd, could sit on *tabourets* in the presence of the king – who of course was seated on a chair.

By the eighteenth century, although the idea of a chair as a symbol of power was still potent, chairs were, in many cases, now also being designed (as opposed to simply evolving) as an integral part of the design and architecture of a house; both William Kent and Robert Adam – the latter usually in collaboration with Thomas Chippendale – produced chair designs for specific rooms in specific houses. There was a new interest in furniture as a statement of style, and

Above left *A modern sofa by Inga Sempe, inspired by mid-century design. The quilted cover softens the angular lines of the frame.*
Above *A variation on Le Corbusier's Grand Confort not, as so often seen, upholstered in leather but in a plain linen, with piping used to accentuate the lines of the chrome frame.*

Above right A vintage sofa – found in a junk shop – is covered in a striking Klein Blue. It looks almost sculptural against the line of the open staircase.

from then on, throughout the nineteenth century style, mainly revivalist in tone, succeeded style: Regency, Victorian gothic – the list goes on, albeit with some interpretations definitely more aesthetically acceptable than others. The end of the nineteenth century picked up an increasingly loud murmur of voices critical of the excessive ornament to be found on much current furniture design. This disaffection presaged groups such as the Arts and Crafts movement, which, in turn, with its emphasis on form following function, was a major intellectual influence on the development of the modernist movement of the early twentieth century.

The twentieth century was without doubt the century of the chair. Designs produced by early modernists such as Walter Gropius, Marcel Breuer, Mies van der Rohe and Le Corbusier were

Left In a corner of a large sitting room and framed against an ornate nineteenth-century painted screen by Edward Burne-Jones (a member of William Morris's Arts and Crafts movement), a chair designed by Carlo Mollino in the 1940s looks remarkably at ease.

Above Looking like a creature from outer space, the Saint James chair by Jean Nouvel has been imaginatively upholstered in apple-green velvet.

extraordinary in their original concept and their innovative use of new technologies and new materials. The chairs produced by a second wave of designers such as Ray and Charles Eames, Verner Panton, Hans Wegner and Eero Saarinen, employing emergent new materials such as fibreglass and moulded plastic, were just as groundbreaking and just as influential – as evidenced by the fact that many of the designs of these talented names are still produced under licence today.

Chairs can play many parts in an interior, all equally important – they can be the casual bystanders, the working participants or the stars of the show. Casual bystanders are the side chairs, the chairs brought out when needed; the participants are those with an everyday purpose, such as dining chairs, armchairs and bedroom chairs. And the stars are – well, it's always pretty obvious when you see them, from whatever century they hail. As far as the last century is concerned, anything by Breuer, Le Corbusier and Mies van der Rohe could be considered to have a starring role, but there are also later unmistakable and striking designs – Arne Jacobsen's 1958 womb-like Egg chair, Verner Panton's 1960s S chair, which looks as if it is coiled ready to spring, and Eero Saarinen's calm and elegant 1956 Tulip chair, possibly the most popular contemporary dining chair of all time. The list goes on, with designers from Europe, the USA and Japan all producing surprising, innovative and beautiful chairs and, as the next pages show, any and all of them will work, and work hard, in an interior, whether it be sleek and modern, vintage and surprising, or classical and cool.

Below left *In a restored cottage, a pair of 1950s armchairs rests against the wall that divides the kitchen from the sitting room.*
Below centre *The famous 1950s Coconut chair by Bertoia is timeless in any setting.*
Below right *A pair of blue upholstered Orange Slice chairs designed by Pierre Paulin in the 1960s.*

From top left to right A metal frame chair from the 1950s in front of a tempera picture by Gerard Drouillet. / In a contrast of textures, a velvet-covered sofa is paired with a cone-shaped chair in cane from the 1950s is paired with a painted, wooden, turned Napoleon III chair. The white cone lamp is vintage, found in a flea market. / A pair of white vintage chairs against a multipatterned tiled background. / Against a cool white background, the white rocking version of the Eames fibreglass DAR chair, launched in 1953.

From left to right Moulded wooden chairs with tubular metal legs work as well on an outside terrace as they do inside the house. / A plastic-covered cone chair in Acapulco yellow both contrasts and harmonizes with yellow-patterned ceramic tiles in a terrace in Tunis. / In this bathroom, treated like a sitting room, a modern chair based on a famous Eames design gives more than a nod to retro style. / A 1950s Finnish carpet in lime-green stripes paired with a re-edition of an Eames chair.

WORKING CHAIRS A good working chair is designed to work hard at many things: at a desk or a table in an office or study of, course, but also at a dining table – indeed, many working chairs are so designed to excel at both. Just because a working chair has a practical purpose, it does not mean that it should not be comfortable, but comfort here does not come through soft upholstery or cushions, but rather its shape. The best of chairs will have been designed to support the body, as well as being easily portable – and also to be, above all, functional (as well as goodlooking of course). The best of modernist retro-style designs are all that anyone could wish for. Many of them are made in materials like moulded plastic or fibreglass, and often with lightweight tubular metal frames and they have a chameleon-like quality, an ability to work easily with everything else in the room. Their clean lines mean that they will sit tight in front of tables and desks, and if the design is one with a single-pedestal base, such as Verner Panton's S chair and Eero Saarinen's famous Tulip chair, they will slide smoothly and discreetly out of sight beneath the table or desk top.

This page In a Paris study, a striking pair of Verner Panton's moulded plastic S chairs, designed in 1960, but looking fifty years younger when accompanied by a classic desk light, the 1970s angular Tizio lamp, which echoes the angles of the chairs.
Opposite, clockwise from top left In a restored house from the 1950s, a study area with the original furniture – a desk chair, and a desk on a pair of integral storage cabinets. / A simple study area with a desk and vintage chair bought on auction site eBay, with metal wall shelves and linen curtains. / A small office on a floor of blue-shaded stone and walls of stone and cement. Against this rough background a pair of metal old school chairs blend in perfectly. / Around a dining table, Alber from India Mahdavi is a set of Chaises Cherner from an antiques market.

STOOLS A rough piece of wood with three legs – or sometimes four – the stool is the earliest form of seating that we know, made and used in many societies and cultures since classical times and still produced in many guises today. Like the wheel, civilized life would have been very different without it – both the turned chair and the Windsor chair, with spindles inserted into the back of the stool, evolved directly from the basic stool. Generally once the lowliest – and lowest – piece of seating that could be imagined, used for such work as milking, and kept in the fireside corner of the kitchen, the stool has also had its grander moments as an instrument of power and status. At the court of Louis XIV, for example, to be seated on an upholstered stool, known as a *tabouret*, was a highly sought-after privilege, and was reserved only for those of noble rank when in the presence of the monarch. A stool can be high for eating – a chrome or wooden-legged bar stool, sometimes with a back rest; or low – like Alvar Aalto's adaptable stacking stool. It can be static, or adjustable; it can be used to rest the feet, to double as a table – it is still indispensable in every situation.

Right *In an eating corner in a Paris flat, made sunny with bright yellow paint, stools by Poltrona Frau covered in yellow leather surround a counter.*

Opposite, clockwise from top left
A kitchen and dining room furnished entirely with vintage pieces, from bar stools to cupboards and hanging lamps. / Moulded polished wooden stools, in a style as timeless as the wheel. / Metal bar stools on angled legs look like small industrial robots. / Vintage round-seated metal stools with an industrial air.

Above left A trio of brightly lacquered tripod tables, with a table lamp by Noguchi; behind is a winged bench lacquered in peacock-blue.

Left A two-part perforated metal table in yellow and grey by Mathieu Matégot, with ceramic pieces by Melanie Cornu.

Above A cord-seated rocking chair on a flat base, with bentwood arms, next to a caned cone chair, around a low square coffee table. The dissimilar shapes of the chairs are united by texture.

Opposite, left A sixties-style sitting corner with a petal-flap table and faux leather armchairs.

Opposite, right In the living room of Gérard Drouillet a metal and glass low table designed by Jean Prouvé is a perfect surface for a collection of brightly coloured ceramics.

OCCASIONAL TABLES

The first tables were cut logs or planks on trestles – sturdy objects that were pretty basic, employed for eating and often brought into use, after any food had been cleared, to sleep on. That developed into the dining table, but the concept of small tables, occasionally holding tea and coffee pots, needlework, books – things, generally – only came into being when domestic life began to move on from the purely practical to embrace the concept of leisure and comfort. Occasional tables have slid in and out of fashion and popularity; illustrations of High Victorian interiors often show sitting rooms so crammed with tables – close by armchairs, lurking in corners, laden behind sofas – that circulation must often have been a most arduous task. Today they are an important element of a living space: they are multifunctional; they are easily moveable; and their decorative qualities, in terms of both ornament and design, are an added bonus. They can be used as punctuation marks in the arrangement of a room, and best of all, the occasional table is an easy way to bring a bit of retro spirit into a room, as it mixes and contrasts so easily with pieces from other periods and styles.

STORAGE

Although it is not very glamorous as a concept in the design spectrum, storage really is one of the most important aspects of contemporary interior design – and, indeed, it always has been. We live in an undeniably consumer society and we love our 'stuff', but most of us have much too much of it and we all need somewhere to keep it, other than in a large box under the bed.

Modernist design was as much about a new way of living as it was about new materials and new technology. Order and efficiency, both inside and outside the building, were part of the make-up of the Bauhaus school of thinking, as was how to design furniture and fittings that would be integral to the living space – as exemplified by Le Corbusier in his writings on the new 'House-Machine'. What we now call open-space living, and how things worked within that space, was part of this new architecture, and a great deal of thought was given to clever, intelligent use of space, from built-in cupboards and shelves with unobtrusive sliding panel doors to beds that dropped down from behind doors, as well as specific designs for specialized storage for everything from books to martini glasses.

But although efficient living and integral storage of all descriptions were part of the broader movement, many of the leaders of the modernist movement were furniture designers, rather than architects, and so often looked for free-standing solutions to the storage conundrum. As well as chairs, there are many serious pieces of furniture to be found from the

Opposite, clockwise from top left An industrial storage unit converted into kitchen storage and dresser top, as part of a kitchen and dining room. / In Gérard Drouillet's apartment, an imposing chest in ebonized oak dating from the 1970s; in front is a pair of twentieth-century leather chairs from Tobia Scarpa. / A removable upholstered banquette sits under a wall of bookshelves and brightly coloured panel units.

Right A free-standing modular storage unit designed by Arnaud Coffort, peopled with toys from the 1920s, a Keith Haring pink dog, tin cans by Andy Warhol and a lamp in the style of Boris Lacroix.
Below A pair of fine eighteenth-century cabinets with linen-fold decoration, one a base for a collection of plaster maquettes by Gio Ponti.

Right A vintage chest of drawers with distressed paintwork.

Below left A rough stone wall, a vintage office plan chest, a 1950s poster of a transatlantic liner and signage form a charming group.

Below right In a dining room in Provence, a stone-topped metal table with an industrial feel has shelves holding local pottery, green glass, baskets and wooden chopping blocks.

Opposite, clockwise from top An industrial trolley acts as a convenient and flexible shelving and storage unit for magazines and books. / A commodious china and glass cupboard, made from a pair of nineteenth-century, glass-panelled doors. / An old, glass-panelled display cabinet is as at home in a domestic context as it would be in a shop.

mid-twentieth century – cupboards, dressing chests and chests of drawers, tallboys, all of them designed for both bedroom and living room; many of these pieces were made in fine woods like walnut, oak, teak and birch, and embellished with veneers and subtle detailing.

And, of course, there was the sideboard – see pages 138–39 – which the designers of the time brought smartly back into the furniture fold after it had languished, unloved, for many years; beautiful, innovative designs were produced and it is no exaggeration to say the super-sleek, low-lying and streamlined look of these pieces still influence furniture design today.

The mid-twentieth century was not of course simply a period of domestic design. Post-war industry and trade demanded pieces of furniture too, designed to fit the bill, whatever that bill happened to be. On the factory floor, in a busy office or store, work-friendly storage was needed, and plenty of it. It might have been industrial metal filing cabinets and file trolleys, or wooden plan and document chests or even shop counters, fixtures and fittings; they were all produced in quantity, and many of these pieces are now being used today as alternative storage ideas in a retro environment. Very much of their time, but obviously not as refined as the more lady-like domestic designs, their slightly rough-diamond image, coupled with chunky solid lines, works very well with other retro styles in every room.

SIDEBOARDS

The late eighteenth century saw the first designated dining rooms – before that, meals were taken at tables set up in other rooms. Some talented cabinet-makers, such as Thomas Chippendale, incorporated a new piece of furniture into the room as part of what might be called the dining room suite. It stood along the wall and incorporated a serving surface with, beneath it, a varying arrangement of drawers and cupboards for silver, china and often wine. Elegant and useful, the sideboard, or credenza, was a perfect example of form and function. A hundred years or so later, sideboards may still have been useful, but they were sturdy and substantial, rather than elegant, and fell from favour, to be revived, however, as a concept but with a slightly different function in the new modernist designs produced during the first part of the twentieth century; form and function was again the theme, and elegance was back. Found in the living room as often as the dining room – if there still was one – these sideboards were often extremely good-looking – low-slung and waist-high, narrow of leg, and full of practical features such as sliding panel doors. They look as good today as they did when they were first designed and have a place in the most eclectic of rooms.

Left The sideboard, along with the other furniture in the room, was made to measure for this house in the 1950s. Behind the sideboard is a wall hanging of the same period by Jean Lurcat.
Below left A 1950s sideboard designed by Florence Knoll, embellished by a 1940s ceramic piece by Chomo.
Below centre A sideboard designed by the celebrated designer T.H. Robsjohn-Gibbings in 1955; behind, a pair of photographs by Vik Muniz.
Below Guarded by a tasteful penguin found at auction is a vintage sideboard with sliding panelled doors.
Opposite In artist Gérard Drouillet's home, two of his canvases are hung above a strong, simple wooden sideboard designed by Charlotte Perriand in the 1930s.

Lighting

Along with scale and proportion, lighting is one of the most important elements in any interior design scheme – some might say the most important. Before the advent of gas and, later, electricity, interiors were lit by oil lamps or candles, and many early twentieth-century lamp designs simply reproduced the forms of the familiar sconces, candelabra and chandeliers, substituting candle-shaped bulbs for the real thing. But by the mid-twentieth-century, electric lighting was a common enough concept for designers to see lighting design as a liberation – an opportunity to experiment with the new materials and technologies that were employed in architecture and furniture design. It was an exciting new field and imagination and innovation went hand in hand, producing altogether new designs in metal, plastic, fibreglass and real glass; they were geometric and angular, undulating and rounded, and they exploded from ceilings, unfolded from walls, sprouted from tables and rose from the floor, many of them close to sculpture. Not only did these mid-twentieth-century lights pave the way for the ever more innovative and experimental forms that were to follow, but, – as evidenced by the fact that many of the original designs are still produced – they are among the most adaptable of retro designs and take their place with ease in spaces of other periods and styles.

Above *A dining alcove of a small apartment, with a black metal lamp from the 1950s on a Danish sideboard and a multicoloured pendulum light designed by Lunel in 1960.*
Above right *Beside a cluster floor lamp from the 1950s is a rocking version of an Eames chair from 1953. Careful consideration has been given to the grouping of objects in this corner of the room.*

Opposite *A dining corner of this large living room features a Knoll table, Series 7 chairs by Arne Jacobsen and a floor lamp, Pêches de Nuit by Pascal Mourgue, hanging over the table.*

CEILING LIGHTS

There are certain rooms that simply do not work without some sort of pendulum light – tall rooms, obviously, but also rooms of perfect proportions that need varying focal points. The ceiling, unsullied except occasionally by moulding and cornice, is a fine background for a bravura light (although not for a flex and a bulb dangling limply from above). Designers and architects have always known this – in the eighteenth and nineteenth centuries, candlelight, for example, was dramatically enhanced when seen through the prisms of chandeliers, those incredibly beautiful glass-hung necklaces and tear drops of light. The modernist designers of the twentieth-century were no less enthusiastic – the idea of a bold, clean background against which a dramatic lamp could be hung was embraced enthusiastically from the 1930s onwards. Pendulum lights were produced that were *tours de force* in terms of imagination and innovation. Some designs were almost free-form, others incredibly disciplined, and inspiration was taken from nature as well as the increasingly accessible world of science. These ideas, combined with new materials and construction technologies, resulted in lights that work as well today as they did seventy or so years ago, and which can be happily used in conjunction with contemporary lighting and furniture.

Opposite A huge, curving, multi-petalled flower of a light, Discoco, designed by Christophe Matthieu In 2008, dominates this bedroom.

Above left Circles of white following circles of white, with a Ball chair designed by Eero Aarnio in the 1960s placed almost as if beneath a globe of paper stars.

Above right Scheisse, a contemporary pendant light looming almost like a giant broken bulb suspended in the air; sculptural in appearance, it hangs over an all-white kitchen table and white moulded plastic chairs.

Left In the kitchen, a ceramic white sink is set into an old shop counter, with two vintage enamelled lemon-yellow metal lamps hanging above.
Opposite Original and charming, a row of hanging ceramic lamps, designed as oversized, upside-down tea cups, form a quirky accent.

Right On a tongue-and-groove panelled wall, an angle lamp of retro design frees up space in the room.

Far right In a rural finca, a dramatic yet practical lighting scheme, using angled ceiling lamps by Flos, illuminates the simple dining table with its distinctive metal chairs.

Below left An oversized adjustable and extended chrome and steel lamp of classic design swings out from the dining room wall.

Below right A typical, cone-shaped wall lamp directed into the bedroom. Its strong colour makes it stand out as a feature.

WALL LIGHTS

WALL LIGHTS For many people, the choice of wall light is a hard one, because the right design depends so much on whether the light is needed as a background ambient light, a decorative element of a larger scheme, or whether there is work to be done – perhaps illuminating a pathway between two points or used as a task light, directing a specific beam on a table or worktop. Whatever the requirements, however, they are probably not best served by a faux traditional solution, such as a decorative sconce that might once have held candles or even a pair of flaming torches.

Retro wall light designs were divided pretty distinctly into the decorative and the practical. Many of the task light designs were based on the idea of adjustable angles or extensions that could be altered to focus on a particular point. Other designs were created for their beauty – a combination of glass, chrome and other materials, coupled with a light source, all coming together to form a sculptural piece; art on a wall that embellished the room but also acted as a further layer of background lighting highlighting the furniture, the pictures and the smaller table lights. It was a sophisticated concept.

Above left *A pair of rare vintage coloured glass wall lights that look like clumps of icicles.*
Above right *A trio of fluorescent column wall lamps, which, although of new design, are very much in line with retro styling with their chrome finish.*

FLOOR LIGHTS

During the 1960s and 1970s, floor lights – or standard lamps as they were then also known – were deemed unfashionable, due in all probability to the then ubiquitous lamp style of an upended, sometimes frilly, flowerpot balancing on a stick that could be found in living rooms up and down the country. But there were always handsome twentieth-century floor lamps out there, many of them designed during the 1950s, it was just that they were, on the whole, unloved. Happily, that prejudice has now been overturned and we are able to see those lamps in a different light, so to speak – to see them for what they are – useful and often very good looking, sculptural and dramatic, and valuable additions to any room. On a practical level, they are without peer – easily portable on slender unobtrusive stems and able to direct light to a particular spot such as a reading chair or dining table, or placed in a semi-permanent position that could not easily be lit by other forms of lighting. Some, like the majestic Arco lamp, an aluminium arc embedded in a chunk of marble and designed in 1962 by Achille Castiglioni, have been classics ever since they were first produced; others have been discovered or rather rediscovered. All of them work today.

Above left In a large Paris apartment, a striking large floor lamp designed by Lunel in the 1950s.
Above A dining area in a large living space filled with a circular table and chairs by Eero Saarinen, illuminated, as well as decorated, by a multi-angled lamp from Jieldé.
Opposite There is a sculptural allure in a tripod light like this Mante Religeuse – or Praying Mantis – designed by Rispal in the 1950s.

TABLE LAMPS

In the design world, table lamps can sometimes be perceived as displaying the more feminine side of lighting; it is they that sport the pretty shades and the ornamental bases. But not so with the lamps designed by the early modernists. For them, both the table lamp and the desk lamp (all of which were designed with integral shades, usually of metal or glass) were opportunities to experiment with shape and materials; to combine practicality with good looks – form and function at its best. These were designs that were totally new – no throwbacks to candlesticks or oil lamps, and no extraneous ornament. Decoration came through the shape of the base and the often contrasting shape of the shade. In the 1930s an automotive engineer, George Carwardine, invented and designed the Anglepoise lamp, which was supported and balanced by a sequence of springs; still in production today, it inspired, both then and now, possibly more variations on a theme than any other desk lamp ever. As lighting design evolved through the twentieth century, table lamps became more colourful, light-hearted even, with new materials such as Perspex and plastic used in ingenious and clever ways. Many of them were far more suited to be seen as stand-alone pieces than as an accessory or accompaniment to other objects.

Below left A version of Verner Panton's Panthella table lamp, first designed in 1971. It looks as modern as it did forty years ago.
Below A new lamp but very much in vintage style – elegant, sharp and witty at the same time.
Opposite The cone-shaped shade was first popularized in the 1950s and has been produced repeatedly in many versions ever since.

Opposite An intriguing combination of texture and pattern, one laid on top of the other. On an intricate tiled floor, a Berber kelim rag rug is draped over a simple contemporary sofa. A standard chrome lamp from the 1970s stands against the wall beneath an open staircase designed by the owner.

Right Textiles rule in this intriguing room: a panther print covers the window, the vintage armchair (where it is combined with a cheerful crocodile print) and even the table, which has a printed panther surface.

Textiles

In the late nineteenth century, the work of William Morris and the Arts and Crafts movement reignited an interest in weaving and textile design. Momentum continued into the next century, and included the influential work of the artists at the weaving workshop at the Bauhaus, where such now-well-known textile designers as Gunta Stolzl and Anni Albers both taught students and created their own original and innovative pieces, following the same principles as other designers associated with the Bauhaus – the aim being to create well-designed pieces that would be available to everyone.

Geometric and abstract patterns, simplified and stylized motifs based on animal, bird and plant life, these designs were striking, bold and, above all, stylish, in a range of colours that ranged from the bright to the subtle; all very different from the popular textile designs of fifty years earlier. Over the next fifty years, other names, from Marion Dorn to Lucienne Day, brought good textile design into the field of general interior design, and so influential were they that some of their furnishing fabric designs – those of Lucienne Day, for example – have been reissued for today's interiors and naturally work extremely well with other elements of retro-style design.

Left and above The owner of this newly built house in Morocco collects rugs, and also liberally spreads one upon another in multicoloured layers in a shaded courtyard where vintage plastic stools and a table provide an interesting contrast in textures.

RUGS In the disciplined, stripped-back modernist interiors of the early twentieth century, rugs played a large part on the often near-bare floors of the new open-plan spaces and it was therefore important that they should be in keeping, and in harmony, with the other elements in the room. They are, after all, the paintings of the decorative art world and make inevitably strong statements in any interior design scheme, in a way that a furnishing fabric, inevitably more incidental, cannot.

Rug design in the first half of the twentieth century, with its bold, eye-catching, geometric and abstract patterns and subtle use of colour, was, not unnaturally, influenced by the work of the Bauhaus and its famed textile department, where both rugs and wall hangings were produced. But beyond the immediate confines of the Bauhaus, there were other designers such as Marion Dorn and Eileen Gray, just as talented and just as influential at the time, whose remaining works are still collected and, in the case of Eileen Gray, reproduced today. If rugs of the period are not to your taste, there are many contemporary designs that will work – just choose one that neither fights nor is subdued by the rest of the décor.

Above left In a streamlined room, with furniture by Christian Liaigre, a striking oval rug of strong pattern from Fedora Design.
Above right A traditional, knotted long-pile Scandinavian Rya rug dating from the 1970s with a re-edition of La Chaise by Charles and Ray Eames.

Left In a corner of the living room, a small vintage cupboard with sliding doors on a 1950s geometrically patterned rug and and a vintage stool covered in a retro-style fabric.
Opposite A bedroom in the pastel tones of the 1950s with a chest of drawers that picks up the pastel turquoise of the bed cover from Woolworths. A rug in cherry and cream blocks adds a touch of sharpness.

FURNISHING FABRICS
Very like the rug designers and weavers of the period, textile designers specializing in furnishing fabrics represented the changing face of post-war design. Again, the textile workshops of the Bauhaus were influential – although they produced woven textiles, their use of colour and their innovative abstract and geometric designs had a strong influence on those designers who were working with printed fabrics. The first designs were largely abstract and geometric, but designers soon began to move towards stylized plant and flower forms, designs that now seem very much of their time. One of the best-known and most representative designers of the period, and still influential today, was Lucienne Day. Married to the equally well-known furniture designer Robin Day, she designed fabrics for progressive companies such as Heal's and produced one design, Calyx, for the Festival of Britain in 1951, which is still in production today. Furnishing fabrics are one of the easiest ways to enter the retro world; not only are the patterns and citrus-sharp colours relatively easy to work into a decorative scheme, but many of the original patterns and designs are still produced and easy to find today.

Surfaces

One of the watchwords of modernism was simplicity at all levels of design, including the reduction or, indeed, elimination of excess surface ornamentation. That did not of course mean that decoration on surfaces was completely banned, but there was certainly a call for cleaner, more graphic decoration where such was required, rather than jungles of swirling foliage climbing its way over everything in a room.

Floors, in particular, were under scrutiny: they could be plain – made of wood, laid with tiles or even the new material linoleum (particularly effective in white). But since the choice of flooring can make a room shrink or widen as it visually reorganizes the space, it was often considered preferable to break up any large area of floor space with areas of clean, geometric pattern, either in the form of rugs defining different areas, as we have seen, or with tiles used in designs of varying scale according to how much space required covering. These simple, usually geometric, designs also showed off the clean lines of the furniture to good effect, and it is that same good effect that should be striven for in a contemporary setting where retro pieces are used today.

Opposite A nineteenth-century, elaborately detailed oak parquet floor seen through the dark Perspex seat of the Ava chair by Song Wen Zhong.
Above left In a carefully restored 1920s villa, a hall with a black-and-white cement floor, treated and coloured to look like stone.

Above left This mosaic-tiled floor in a peacock tail design dating from the 1920s has been lifted, restored and reinstalled in a fine art deco mansion on the Atlantic coast of France.
Above right In a bathroom, a black-and-white Bisazza mosaic tile floor both complements and contrasts with a bathroom table with a ceramic surface.

Left *Hexagonal tiles in a subtle combination of mustard and blue make an interesting background to a vintage bath of classic shape.*
Below left *In a small bathroom, the restored and painted antique bath is lined up against a wall of cement tiles.*
Right *The classic design of these eighteenth-century Portuguese azulejos (ceramic tiles) means that they will never date and they will look good wherever they are laid, as here in a small kitchen.*
Opposite *A kitchen furnished in retro style is decorated with a traditional pattern of tiles, used here as a panel that runs behind both the sink and the preparation area.*

WALL TILES
For hundreds of years, wall tiles have been an important part of the story of decorative art, both reflecting and complementing the styles of the time, a role they still hold today They also of course have a practical purpose – installed behind a bath or basin, or as a splashback behind a kitchen sink, where they can add a robust accent of decoration to a functional room. The first part of the twentieth century, when overblown pattern was less popular, and geometric and abstract designs were seen as being more of the time, the design of wall tiles followed the trend and became more restrained.

Today, the range of pattern available is once again both wide and broad, and pretty much anything goes, so an element of informed choice is required when pairing wall tiles with furniture or art that could be considered retro style. This does not mean sticking to plain or geometric patterns – far from it; many of the more traditional tiles go extremely well with twentieth-century design. The key is not to overload, to use the tiles as another element of the decoration rather than as the reason for the room.

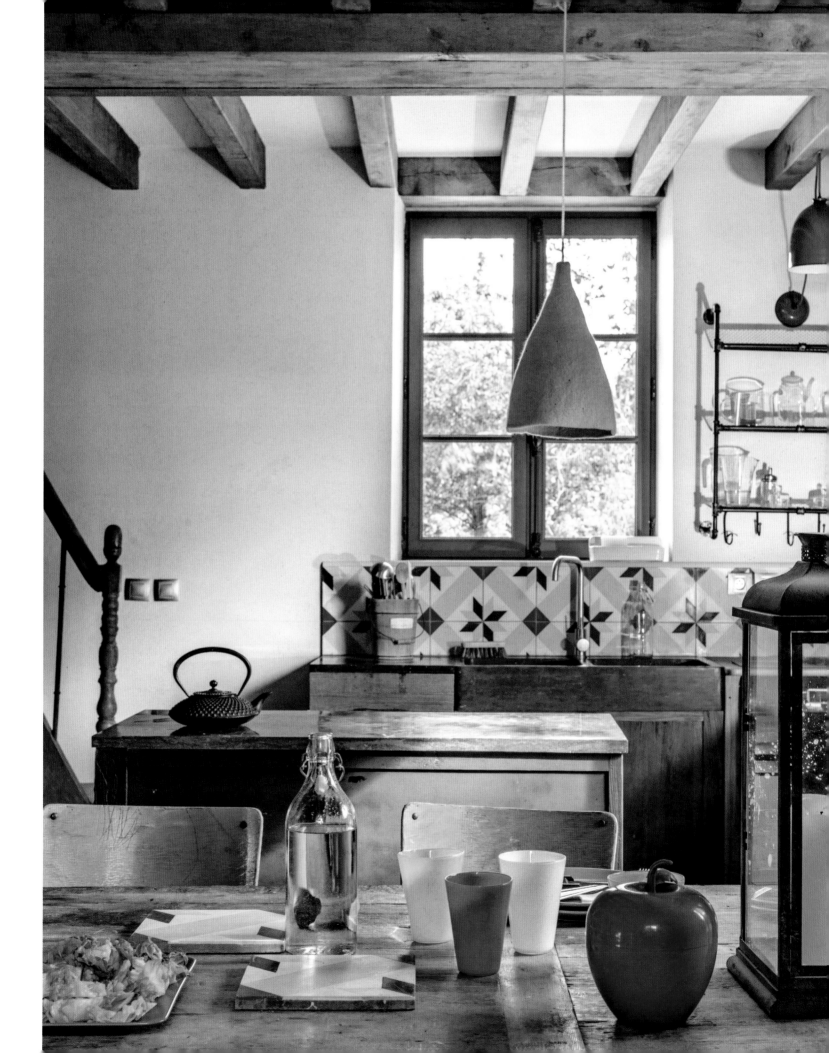

Above left and left The wonderfully original open screen of metal honeycomb structures winds around this innovative house built in the 1950s, including the unusual built-in bar. The screen seems to bring the outside in, and vice versa. This is a house of structure, where the unexpected lies around every corner.

Opposite and above In a building designed in the 1950s, the inner courtyard is decorated with a striking fresco – indeed, an entire colour scheme – painted originally in 1960 by Wilfredo Arçay, a Cuban artist. The piece was restored, using original colours, by L'Atelier du Temps Passé.

PAINT & STRUCTURE
Until the manufacture of paint was industrialized in the nineteenth century the colours that you chose for the walls inside your house were a matter of practicality, but also of income. Some colours such as the stone shades were not only hardwearing and did not fade but they were also relatively cheap; other colours such as reds and yellows were far more expensive and were therefore used only in the houses of those who could afford such style. But by the end of the nineteenth century paint was being mass-produced and from then on a full range of colours was available to all who were interested. The architects and designers and artists of the modernist movement had strong views about colour, and the early work is characterized by black, white and grey with occasional additions of bright primary colour – think Rietveldt and Mondrian; but interest began to grow in the possibilities of colour as life-enhancing as well as a spatial tool, which could be particularly useful in the delineation of specific spaces in the new open-plan living areas. So interested did Le Corbusier himself become in the use of colour that he collaborated with a Swiss paint company to produce two ranges of paints known as the Colour Keyboards, or les Claviers de Couleurs.

Far left A re-edition of a Mauny wallpaper, Les Danseuses, in a small bedroom, furnished with 1930s furniture and decorations.
Left An elegant wallpaper, Le Poète from Mauny, is redolent of the design style of the 1930s and the airy lines of a pair of contemporary wrought-iron beds.
Below left A contemporary trompe l'oeil trellis paper on the walls, in front of which is a nineteenth-century bed, dressed with a pair of tapestry cushions. Against the wall is a pair of 1950s Hans Wegner Wishbone chairs.
Below right A wall that has been totally 'pantherized' – in fact it is not only the wall, but the floor as well; even the bed cover and the linen belong to the panther.

Opposite In a study area, a Sanderson re-edition of a textured wallpaper dating from the 1950s. Every detail has been carefully sourced to be in period, including the ceramic light switch.

FEATURE WALLPAPER

Since the first roll of decorated paper was painstakingly printed several hundred years ago, wallpaper has slid in and out of fashion, always in competition with its rival, paint. Although dismissed as background by some, for others, wallpaper is an important element of the design – a scene-setter for the other elements of the room. Wallpaper was originally produced as a cheap imitative alternative for walls that, in wealthier interiors, might have been hung with woven damasks and velvet or with elaborate hand-painted scenes; but as time went on, as with other once hand-made elements of the interior, gradual industrialization meant that by the end of the nineteenth century, wallpaper was being mass-produced and widely available to all. Many wallpaper companies today have long held archives of both their own designs and also of rediscovered document pieces, which is important when – as now – wallpaper enters one of its fashionable moments. This means that authentic designs from every decade of the twentieth century are now being reproduced, which is excellent news for those who want to completely reproduce a retro-style room, or for those who would simply like to add a touch of twentieth-century chic to an already interesting space.

Decoration

Little things mean a lot, especially in interior decoration terms. Little things in this case are the accessories, the wall art, the ceramics, the bits – these are the cupcakes of life, the interesting things that pull a room together and make you look again at the other elements of the room. These pieces are often the things that give an otherwise near-perfect room its personality and create an atmosphere, something that is not automatically present in a room. It is however not just a question of adding all the things you like into a room; choice is important, of course, but also important is putting things together in the right mix, making sure that the groupings and combinations work. Retro decoration – anything from the 1920s to the 1970s – is an easy-going friend; not only do most twentieth-century pieces work with each other, they also usually work very well with things from other periods and styles. The only rules to remember are those design constants of scale and proportion: a large ceramic charger or bowl will not look well next to a delicate porcelain figurine, nor would a large pop-art poster work against a small black-and-white silhouette.

Opposite, left On a 1950s oak cupboard with sliding doors in lime-yellow, a rattan sunray mirror, with etched orange ceramic jug and beakers and a bird bowl, all lit by a diabolo light from the 1950s.
Opposite, right Pop-art retro style: on the bright yellow fridge a neon-pink framed card from Café Breton and a turquoise-blue-faced clock.

This page A striking, flamboyant wall hanging by Alexander Calder with, in the foreground on a low table, a 1940s ceramic piece by Chomo; all high art, but extremely decorative.

MIRRORS

Mirrors – looking glasses, as they were once, perhaps more accurately, known – are extremely important features in a room, in fact it could be said that a room is incomplete without one. They are useful, of course, in the most practical of senses to check your own image before you face the world. But they are even more useful in decorative terms, where they perform endless miracles, from reflecting other parts of the room to opening up areas, catching light in a dark room and throwing it back and accentuating and giving depth to objects. Although a mirror will always add drama, if it has a striking or beautiful frame, it will make even more of an impression. A group of mirrors hung together, particularly if they are a mixture of both large and small, can bring an almost magical quality to a room, their appearance changing with the changing light. But perhaps their most useful decorative role is one of making other pieces of wall art look better: when they are hung with a diverse collection of other things on the wall, they act like candles or small directional electric lights, highlighting the pictures and objects surrounding them and giving them a new importance.

Opposite, clockwise from left
A formidable sun mirror made at Vallauris in 1950. / A wall of luminous blue-green is hung with old chrome placemats from 1950s bistros; here, they act as mirrors and make a pleasing, light-reflective group. / A collection of witches' mirrors on the top of a bureau, with a lamp from the Singer workshop.

Above left *A wall collection of the iconic mirror design so beloved of the 1950s – the sun in all its risings. Surrounded by other objects and pictures, the composition is a pleasing one.*
Above right *Ornately framed mirrors hung on either side of a narrow corridor emphasize the amusing contemporary silhouette, in the style of Aubrey Beardsley, painted onto the panels of the front door.*

WALL ART

Wall art is what it says – not just the conventional idea of pictures in frames, but anything that can either be hung on a wall or that looks better on a wall – not necessarily the same thing! If your taste is towards a modernist or retro interior, or if you have a combination of styles used together, it is important that whatever is on the wall is clean and collected. It is also important that it or they are hung in a manner that makes the most of the art and the most of the room. A large picture or a bold picture is usually best hung in relative isolation, with enough space around it for it to, metaphorically, breathe. Pictures that have a common theme or that are in a common medium – photography, perhaps, or monotone prints – often look better if they are hung as a group or, at any rate, in relatively close proximity to each other. Small pictures, even if they share no discernible theme, can be made into a pleasing collection of shapes and colours and hung as such. As always, the answer is to make sure that the room or space works as a whole rather than a series of disjointed snapshots.

Opposite, clockwise from top left *A collage, Rolling Stones VI by Raymond Hains, above a sideboard, ornamented with a Bibibibi lamp by Ingo Maurer. / A leather sofa of classical twentieth-century lines by Berge Morgensen underneath a collection of black-and-white photos and prints that work together because they are all monochrome in tone. / A group of disparate objects ranging from African figures, zinc architectural shapes and two of a triptych hung low.*
Right *In this nineteenth-century apartment, a striking work by Pierre Dimitrienko more than holds its own hung on a panelled wall.*

Above left With their backs to an ornate gilded mirror, a pair of stuffed parrots survey the scene from their marble mantelpiece perch.

Above right A plaster bust of Queen Hedwig Eleonore of Sweden and blue-and-white bowls stand beneath an old teaching chart.

OBJETS D'ART

The middle of the twentieth century was a period when studio ceramics and glass enjoyed great popularity, and artists and designers in Europe and America produced a wide variety of pieces that reflected the fashions and interests of the times. Like *objets d'art* of other eras and periods, these twentieth-century pieces can stand alone if they are visually arresting and strong enough in shape, colour and concept, but they can also be combined with other interesting objects that work together – not necessarily of the same style or even of the same period. The important thing is to display such pieces in

Above A representative collection of retro ceramic pieces – brightly coloured designs from Vallauris, Capron and Baudart.
Above right Although contemporary, this earthenware pichet, designed and made by Gérard Drouillet, is much influenced by pieces made by artists of the mid-twentieth century.
Right On the shelf is a 1950s vase deppicting a Siren and a red, three-dimensional comma. On the lower shelf, a print by Claire Lavallée.

a manner that will draw attention to them – in a good way – and highlight the decorative or artistic qualities of each piece. Finding the right base and the right background for any piece is important, as otherwise no matter how beautiful an object, it might languish away for lack of focus; some large pieces may be able to stand on their own in the centre of a room, but most objects and ornaments look better against something. A mantelpiece – particularly if there is an overmantel mirror – is a tried-and-tested traditional choice, and none the worse for that, but a simple wall can work just as well in terms of the overall effect.

ROOM BY ROOM

Incorporating the look throughout the house

Below left *Furniture of the mid-twentieth century goes so well with newer pieces that it is easy to see the evolutionary progression of style. At one side of this totally contemporary room sits a Charles Eames DAR chair with arms, first produced in the early 1950s.*
Below centre *Retro style even works in the mountains: retro metal all-purpose Tolix chairs covered in warm sheepskins, take on a comfortable, even cosy, appearance.*

Below right *The best designs of the period were supremely adaptable. Here as a desk/dressing chair is an armless Eames chair that fits into the room like a glove.*
Opposite *A stripped-back dining room in which the retro pieces – chairs – can shine. On a floor of stained oak is the simplest of tables: Pixels de Mer by Christian Nesler. The vintage chairs are a classic shape of the 1960s, and the tableau is completed by a still life by Kevin Best.*

RETRO STYLE – twentieth-century design – is the broadest of churches, and that is one of its joys; from the almost stately designs of the early masters like Le Corbusier, Charles and Ray Eames and Alvar Aalto to the bouncing, bubbly pop-art explosions of the 1970s, the range of styles, materials, shapes and colours is both wide and deep.

When many of these pieces were designed in the first half of the twentieth century the traditional arrangement of interior space – several different rooms each with a single function – was changing into a looser pattern, described at the time as open-plan living, and the new furniture designs fitted perfectly into this modern modus vivendi. The pieces were adaptable – they could often be used or repeated from room to room – as well as comfortable and, most important, fit for purpose. Form and function was the design watchword of the age, after all.

Today, the range of retro styles and designs that can still be found is far-reaching and can be incorporated into every room, including the bathroom. But they can't just be plonked down anywhere – incorporating retro pieces into the home requires some thought, for although Mies van der Rohe – another of the earlier masters of twentieth-century design – used the phrase, 'Less is More' in relation to architecture, it also applies to how few or how many retro pieces can be used in a room or, indeed, in a larger space, and before any decision is made, it is wise to do a bit of planning.

And that is where this book can help: in this section – indeed, throughout the book – we have chosen homes where clever placing and intelligent spacing make every element – retro and contemporary, antique and modern – work together in original and innovative settings.

Living spaces

The sort of room in which retro pieces look most at home are what might be called, in other contexts, living rooms, but which are, generally speaking, so much more. Like every other room in the contemporary house, the whole function of the modern living room has changed almost beyond recognition since the 1950s.

Once upon a time, the living room, or sitting room, was a very distinct and distinctive area – it had not become the catch-all space it so often is today. Then it was a place for leisure, usually leisure that was more sedentary than not, and it was home to relatively peaceful pursuits. Today, the living room is often a much larger, open-plan space, part sitting room, part working room, a bit of a reading room and often a bit of a viewing room; it is a space in which not only specific functions take place, but which is flexible enough to absorb other activities and occupations, whatever they may be.

But however much these rooms have changed in appearance, what hasn't changed are the abiding principles of good interior design – proportion, scale and balance. These are still as paramount and important as they ever were.

The concept of scale and balance became an element of interior design at around the time people started to think about what might make a room look and feel good, rather than simply fulfil a utilitarian

Opposite The modern sofa is draped with an antique, dyed, sheet. The open-weave bucket chairs are a twentieth-century design staple.
Right A serene sitting room furnished with vintage pieces of different styles that work together through colour and texture. Panelled wooden walls, which have been limed, and a painted wooden floor are the background for an intricate slotted table, an armchair and a classic Gras lamp.

purpose. Before the Industrial Revolution and the advent of mass production, furniture was – as it were – made to order, usually from a cabinet-maker or through an architect. As always, the owner's status and wealth were designed to be reflected through his new furniture but also, now, his refinement and taste were to be seen through his choice of style, which is where the idea of a pleasing and harmonious combination of line and shape became important.

And it remains so today: we have all experienced that vaguely unsettled, but indefinable feeling of discomfort that one gets in certain rooms; everything seems just a little out of kilter and slightly uncomfortable, and the cause is usually because the room is unbalanced or out of proportion. It is not a question of everything matching – far from it – but it is a question of everything going together. So choosing the right pieces of furniture and accessories – particularly for a living room – is terrifically important, which is why introducing something from another time, style or period is so helpful. It adds an individuality and an interest that lifts the room and makes it work as a welcoming and functional space.

Right In Tunis, a high-ceilinged room opens from the terrace. Designed as a library and a living room, the space is kept deliberately cool and clean with tiles dominating the decoration – even the solitary carpet echoes the floor-tile design. In front of a tall bookcase is a leather and oak sofa by Hugues Chevalier. A pair of armchairs is inspired by the 1950s, and a console and small table are in lacquered metal.

Below At the opposite end of the same room, a matching bookcase takes up the far wall. In front of the television, a leather chair from Habitat, again influenced by 1950s design. The amphora-like resin floor lamp is designed by Christophe Pillet.

Furniture and lighting from the mid-twentieth century work well when mixed with other styles precisely because they were designed with functionalism in mind. The ideas and beliefs behind the modernist movement of the 1920s, as exemplified by the Bauhaus school, founded in 1919 with Walter Gropius as its first director, were experiments in meeting the post-war challenge of using the new techniques and materials that were then being developed, to design good-looking furniture that could be easily mass-produced and that would be equally easily available for all to buy. This new technology gave the designers and architects of the period an artistic freedom, untrammelled by what had gone before, to move away from the conventional and to design pieces that would be ready for the future.

Although a few modernist pieces – the classic star-turn designs from the first masters, perhaps – look well on their own, relatively isolated and metaphorically spotlit, the majority of retro pieces need no such isolation. In fact, they work better as helpmates – and in the rooms shown in this section, it is noticeable that almost every piece has been carefully and intelligently chosen to work with other, sometimes very different, periods and styles. Many of the designs have almost semi-organic shapes, which work in a subtle way to look right wherever they are, particularly when paired with designs which are more geometric in appearance.

The trick to mixing periods and styles and coming up with a homogenous and pleasing whole is to look first at shape and then at scale and proportion. Twentieth-century pieces work so well in twenty-first-century rooms because they have a flexibility and lightness of touch – two elements that are so important in interior design.

Left *A room of colour and contrast: the circular table and matching chair are by Warren Platner, the chair covered in fabric from Designers Guild, and the curtains, also Designers Guild, are Madras silk. By the window, is a 1950s Danish teak tallboy, and a yellow Eames chair sits on a multicoloured, crazy-paving rag rug. The final touch by the fire is a 1950s standard lamp with polychrome cone shades.*

Opposite *In a library, a long Napoleon III sofa has been covered in a soft terracotta with linen-covered cushions, picking up the colours of the photograph by Susan Wides on the wall. The circular coffee table is a 1950s design, and the leather chair, also vintage, was found in a local flea market.*

This page In this grand living room, once a ballroom, and beneath a suitably ornate nineteenth-century cornice and mouldings, vintage furniture of the twentieth century and contemporary pieces hold their own. Leather sofas and stools mix with buttoned leather chairs by Patricia Urquiola for Moroso. Behind the sofa, a pair of vintage blue armchairs and, on the wall a screen of small convex mirrors, found in a flea market.

Left An open sitting room with a large chimneypiece in a Moroccan tadelakt plaster finish, a curved leather sofa dating from the 1970s and a metal-legged table from the 1950s. On a Moroccan rag rug is a white leather Moroccan pouffe.

Below In South Africa, a sunlit room facing the sea, with grey-painted beams and a graphic mix of colours and styles, filled with objects and furniture collected from local sale rooms and antique dealers. Facing the all-white sofa, a pair of 1950s armchairs re-covered in a bright print and a vintage round table in cane and glass.

Opposite In a Tunisian palace, now carefully restored, an airy living room is furnished with an eclectic mix. Sofas and matching chairs upholstered in wool and with lacquered beech legs are 1950s style. The high ceilings and ornate walls mean that it is important for the furniture and furnishings to balance with simple shapes and calm colours.

Right *In a country house, complete with old limed beams and rough stone walls, what might first appear a rather severe eating area is in fact part of a larger kitchen separated by a wide and long opening. On the far side, the kitchen area; on this side, a table made from old wood, surrounded by a set of one of the versions of the most recognizable of mid-twentieth century designs: the Tulip chair, designed in 1956 by Eero Saarinen.*

Eating and dining

In many ways, the dining room, as such, is not an absolute given. Although we all recognize the term, it is not actually a particularly traditional room – its heyday probably only lasted from about the middle of the nineteenth century to the middle of the twentieth century. Before that, few houses had a dining room as we know it, with its attendant permanent dining table and suite of matching chairs. Eighteenth-century tables, except in the grandest of houses, were of various designs, but usually light, portable and adaptable, designed to be used in different rooms and areas around the house wherever food was to be served. But by the nineteenth century, and certainly by the time Queen Victoria ascended to the throne in 1837, there was, for the middle classes, a new emphasis on the importance of the family unit. A cult of virtuous domesticity and a hardening attitude towards class differences, as well as a fashionable enthusiasm for separate rooms for every house-bound activity, from smoking to reading, combined to introduce the idea of a dedicated dining room – a place used every day and where all family meals were taken in relative, formal privacy.

So it remained until the mid-twentieth century, when two world wars, continuing emancipation and the resultant lack of domestic staff meant that, although dining rooms were still often a fixture in many houses, they had too often become rooms, that were in many

Opposite In a basement, the lack of light has been turned into a positive advantage: the paint on the old school table and the matching – more or less – wood and metal benches has been allowed to rub away into a nicely distressed finish. Not to be outdone, the vintage cupboard sports the same look, and the rubbed blue walls and cracked terracotta tiled floor enhance the atmospheric scene.

Right A charming corner to eat in, which looks as if it has just been thrown together but actually requires taste and skill to get the balance and proportions right. A small table is faced with a high-sided wooden bench on one side, and on the other a traditional metal heart-backed chair and an equally traditional slatted back and seat garden chair. A cane stool makes up the party.

Below right Two different pairs of metal chairs of two different vintages work together around a large old metal table in a cellar dining room, brought up to date with a low-hung, wide-shaded metal lamp and a large red canvas on the wall.

cases cold and silent, used only for Sunday family lunches and special occasions. But smaller houses and a less formal way of life generally meant that things had to change, and over the last seventy-five years we have seen various new ways of solving the where-to-eat conundrum, some easier to apply than others, but all variations on a theme.

In some homes there is still a dining room; it remains a self-contained room, with the table as its centre, but it is now a much warmer, open space. When not set for a meal, the table might have books, flowers and objects on it, and the room itself might have a hybrid personality – a place for eating, but also perhaps a study, a home office, even a reading room. In other homes there is a dining area – a dedicated space, but set in a larger scene, as part of the living room, and designed and decorated to fit in with the larger domestic world, with chairs that can be used in other parts of the room and a multi-purpose, good-looking table. A third variation has, most conveniently for many, the dining room as part of the larger kitchen space – distinct from the cooking and preparation area but not in contest with it. In this option the eating area is usually decorated and furnished very much as an offshoot of the kitchen area – informal and

This page *A kitchen-dining room with, along one wall, a range of Ikea units that have been painted black. In the foreground, the kitchen table, which came out of a nineteenth-century French chateau, is surrounded by an assortment of chairs, of different vintages and styles, all of which work together as they are all of the same height.*

Left Below a raised seating area, a lower dining area with a tiled floor and part-tiled wall. The metal dining table – Big Irony by Maurizio Peregalli – is surrounded with bright coloured chairs by Ricardo Blumer, paired with transparent Perspex chairs – Louis Ghost by Philippe Starck.
Below A semi-industrial setting made bright and congenial with primary-coloured chairs that are traditional in style.

Opposite Through a half-glass door into a dining room, an assortment of vintage chairs, including a yellow sheet-metal chair by Tolix. A bust of Hedwig Eleonore, Queen of Sweden, sits by the window.

comfortable; somewhere for people to sit and chat, eat and drink, or even help with the preparation of the meal.

With the death of the formal dining room, of course came the death – unmourned by many – of formal dining suites, the rectangular table with its matching, high-backed chairs, usually in highly polished wood with upholstered seats. Today's diners like something different: contrasting tables and chairs, interesting textures, surfaces and colour, as well as shapes and materials, and a variety of styles, often used together, which is why incorporating twentieth-century furniture into an interior scheme makes so much sense. First of all, there are the materials. Resin, moulded plastic, fibreglass and metal – all enthusiastically employed by designers and architects in the making of

This page In a large, L-shaped living room, the eating area, which leads out onto a courtyard, has been defined by a simple table made by Capron, surrounded by duo-coloured, faux leather-upholstered chairs. The colours have been carefully chosen to blend with the tones of the sitting area beyond.

Opposite A small eating corner within a larger sitting area, framed by a cross-barred bookcase used to display a collection of objects and pictures. A collection of mercury glass balls sits in the centre of a nineteenth-century table, with reeded legs and claw feet. The dining chairs, with tapered legs, are an elegant design from the 1950s

both tables and chairs – are hard-wearing and, on the whole, light enough to be easy to move around, which is important in an area with a working element to it. Then there's the question of colour. Chairs made in moulded plastic and resin, in particular, were produced in a range of bright colours as well as black and white, and so are ideal to add a flash of unexpected colour, particularly in a room where many of the elements may be in neutral tones.

Then there are the inviting shapes – sinuous, rounded, angular, bulbous – which are always interesting. Retro furniture is unexpected in the best possible way – original, quirky and fun, as well as being sometimes extremely elegant. Retro chairs and tables have chameleon characteristics and fit in, as these pages show, in every kind of interior, either mixed with other pieces of the same vintage or used to spike a scheme that is far more traditional in tone.

Above In a rotunda leading from a larger room, a table by Eero Saarinen for Knoll, with chairs by Warren Platner, designed in the early 1960s. The flute-like chandelier is a 1960s design, found in a theatre in Germany.
Above right In a room with a beamed ceiling lined with cane, a zinc table with almost column-like heavy wooden legs makes a strong contrast with the set of shiny white chairs by Paula Navone.

Opposite The house in Royan, designed by Marmouget (see page 76) in the 1950s, and accurately restored and renovated, features a free-standing fire with an impressive conical beaten copper hood and a circular stone hearth. The dining table and set of chairs are of the same period.

Clockwise from top left Traditional
French metal garden furniture in all
its different forms will always work
everywhere, especially when painted in
bright and contrasting colours. / In a
shaded Moroccan courtyard, welcoming
moulded plastic stools and chairs are
light enough to be easily moved around
the space. / Plastic-coated, cone-
shaped chairs make a colourful bunch
on the terrace beside a converted
Provençal mas. / In an old barn, part of
an old Provencal mas, the stone arched
entrance has been enclosed in glass.
The interior, with its cobbled floor, is
furnished with traditional metal folding
chairs and simple trestle tables.

OUTDOOR LIVING

An outdoor space is where everyone wants to be when the sun is shining and the weather is warm. Welcoming, friendly and inviting, outdoor living might take place on an open terrace or a swathe of green grass. It could be beneath a shaded pergola or in a roofed-over area, and it might be a dining space or a sitting and lounging sort of thing. But whatever form the outdoors takes, it should above all be comfortable – made for lazing about or doing something much more energetic, like eating or drinking. Numbers fluctuate out of doors – two can become six or ten in the blink of a butterfly's eye – so it is always important to have enough tables and chairs for everyone to just sit and just be. That is why outdoors is the perfect place to display and use interesting and even unusual pieces of furniture – a home for that which is quirky, fun and a find, plus some easy stacking or folding pieces that wait their turn at the side.

Here is where vintage one-offs, irresistible flea market finds and individual modern pieces can shine. Wood has a natural affinity with the wider outdoors and so always works, so too does the traditional nineteenth- and twentieth-century metal chair and round table. But look also at the variety of synthetic materials that are used in retro twentieth-century design; these are also heaven-sent for outdoor use. Glass fibre, moulded plastic and plastic-coated pieces – ranging from the fairly to the totally indestructible – are both comfortable to sit on and easy on the eye, and it is amazing what a brightly coloured chair or two can bring to the party.

Above A platform in a town garden, designed as a deck for enjoying the sun and also as a shelter when necessary. Vintage white-painted Adirondack chairs wait invitingly.
Far left In the winter garden of a Provençal bastide, an old table is dressed with vintage fabrics and surrounded with restored Thonet chairs, painted soft green. A metal chandelier hanging from a beam is garlanded with trailing greenery.
Left Traditional Provence, where lunch is taken under a pergola of wisteria and vines, and where vintage metal and wood chairs run down a simple table of wooden boards.

Bedrooms

Historically, the bedroom evolved out of man's growing need for privacy. Over the centuries, the room began to be associated with the idea of sanctuary and relaxation – a place that was separated from the more purposeful, or at least busier, life of the rest of the home.

The bed was once one of the most important items of furniture in the house – always mentioned in inventories and often in wills. Large, imposing, often dressed with costly hangings, there was no ignoring it and, in that respect, some things never change, for whether your bedroom is large or small, it will always be dominated by the bed. And the question is always how to humanize it and how to make the bedroom a room that works as more than just a sleeping pod.

The most successful bedroom schemes seem to be those that are light and cheerful and which have an element of the sitting room about them – think eighteenth- and nineteenth-century boudoirs, which were comfortable and well-appointed private sitting rooms for their owners. In the modern bedroom the bed, and bedhead, if there is one, should be in harmony with the rest of the room, and the rest of the room should contain things that are pleasing to live with. There may be a small, slightly delicate desk

Opposite *A bedroom of mixed styles and design, from the bedside tables to the low wooden, African chair and the distinctive sunray mirror. The plain white walls and sheer white curtains on a slim pole hold the disparate elements together.*

This page *A room under the eaves is always a difficult decorating proposition. Here the problem has been solved by making the angled wall into what is almost a full-scale bedhead in wide stripes of red, black and white. The colour theme is continued in the bedcover, the carpet and rugs and even the moulded Verner Panton S chair by the bed.*

Left A door frame found on a building site and then lacquered in grey is re-purposed as a headboard, set against wide-striped grey and white walls and grey linen.

Below left The vintage metal lamps hanging from the beams make a strong contrast against the whitewashed beams and walls.

Below A simply furnished bedroom with old polished floor boards is in keeping with the bathroom behind the pillar. An antique chest by the bed and a wide-seated country chair are all the furniture required. The tall, black, metal angled reading lamps are both practical and elegant.

perhaps, a comfortable chair or even a small sofa, as well as room for books and other bits, for this is an area where pieces and decorative objects that have a personal appeal can be usefully employed, and where pieces from different periods may be mixed together, as long as the scale – ever important – is compatible. Seriousness is not a necessary quality in a bedroom; the decorative element might be colourful, unusual, frivolous even – an adjective that could well describe much of retro accessory design. Ceramics, glass and light fittings designed in the mid-twentieth century were often decorative and quirky in concept; individual in taste and personal in style. Use these colourful pieces liberally – they will be quite at home here, particularly when combined with other, equally individual pieces from other periods.

Opposite In Tunis, a master bedroom, with its tiled walls and ornate painted ceiling, is relatively simply furnished, using flashes of sunshine-yellow – in rugs, chairs and even an oversized self-portrait by David Bowie, which stands out against the patterned wall.

Right A ceiling of stars in a midnight-blue sky, a bed with a painted wooden baroque bedhead surmounted by a circular witch's mirror decorated with peacock feathers; a vintage metal stool at the end of the bed, a silhouette painted on the door, and a chandelier made from wooden toy soldiers. This is real eclecticism.

Left *Overblown grey roses on the wall with an antique Swedish grandfather clock, a striped linen bedcover and black and yellow silk curtains all make for a retro-style room that is absolutely new.*
Opposite *In a bedroom of a restored 1950s house, lemon-yellow walls set the scene. A roll-top shutter conceals shelves in a storage cupboard and the beds are covered in a vintage fabric dating from the same period.*

Bathrooms

Much in the world of bathrooms has changed in the last fifty years. More efficient? Most people would say so. Better-looking? Depends on what you are after. More comfortable? Well, that depends on your definition of comfortable; it does sometimes seem, perhaps, that the more sophisticated and technologically advanced the bathroom becomes, the more slick and savvy it appears. Sometimes personality is lost in the quest for the latest rain forest multi-showerhead, sauna/spa bath, waterproof televisions and hands-free taps. In fact, many bathrooms, once you get past the technology, are really rather dull, not to say impersonal, and most of them would greatly benefit from a softening influence – and not just in the water.

Old basins and baths that have been restored can still be found and are often of far more generous proportions than their contemporary counterparts. Traditional chairs too can work well – a comfortable

Above *A clever combination of industrial and feminine style. Original, restored cement tiles, and an old chest made into a basin unit are combined with a delicate crystal-drop chandelier.*
Above right *Twentieth-century glass wall and pendulum lights make a strong statement that works well in an ultra-modern, clean-lined white and chrome bathroom.*

Opposite *A pleasing mix of styles and periods. On a poured cement floor, the comfortably large basin dates from the 1960s and above it hangs an eighteenth-century mirror of Venetian glass, flanked by two hooded contemporary metal wall lights. An industrial metal stool is a useful addition.*

Left The Zellige tiles, made of clay and coloured glass, produce a translucent, watery effect around the basin in this glamorous bathroom. Hanging from the tiles, a vintage Venetian glass mirror and a bright sunray mirror stand out above the double sinks.
Below Sunshine-orange, a shade readily identifiable with the 1950s, colours this bathroom down to the rolls of paper. A black-and-white glass mosaic floor by Bisazza acts as a foil to the orange walls and worktop.

upholstered chair is one of the nicest additions to any bathroom that is large enough – its very comforting presence transforms the space into a haven. And if the room is not large enough for a chair, a stool – perhaps a good-looking, old metal one – is a handy piece to have about.

Every bathroom needs at least one mirror – something large and striking – but where mirrors are concerned, the more the merrier; the bathroom is a very good place for a collection of different sizes and shapes. Pictures too are helpful – modern steam extractors mean that all but the most valuable works can be hung on bathroom walls, where they add colour – often lacking – as well as a bit of personality. In fact, bathrooms are definitely places in which to use cheery retro accessories of every description, and every colour, as many of the rooms on these pages demonstrate, so experiment and try out different objects around the room. You may well be surprised.

Opposite, left *Clean lines and basic fittings make a suitable background for an equally clean-lined and simple mid-century bathroom chair in this modern bathroom.*

Opposite, right *There is a combination of rustic and industrial retro chic in this bathroom, furnished with a grey stone sink and a metal filing cabinet, used for storage, against a rough-cast stone wall.*

Right *An unsual painted metal stand supports a modern basin, the sea-green colour echoing the sides and feet of the claw-foot bathtub.*

Left The basin stand made from a vintage distressed metal table contrasts with a contemporary round white basin. The turquoise-patterned cement mosaic tiles are echoed in the decorative, painted wooden shelf.
Below In a restored 1920s villa, this original bathroom features a design of silica tiles in monochrome and squares of glass.
Opposite Rectangles of camaïeux turquoise silica and squares of glass decorate this outdoor shower.

Acknowledgements

Page

1	Stephen Clément, stylist Amandine Schira, architect Pierre Marmouget
2–3	Jean-Marc Palisse, stylist Alix de Dives, architect Christophe Ducharme, www.c-ducharme-architecte.com, designer Jean-Michel Wilmotte, www.wilmotte.com
4-5	Jean-Marc Palisse, stylist Caroline Clavier, architect Lacvivier & Limal, designer Florence Lopez, www.florencelopez.com
6	Nicolas Millet, stylist Noémi Barré, designer Frank Schmidt
7	Nicolas Millet, stylist Amandine Schira, architects Arnaud Lacoste and Jérôme Vinçon www.lode-architecture.com
8	Nicolas Mathéus, stylist Laurence Dougier
9	Nicolas Mathéus, stylist Laurence Dougier, architect Antonio Virga, www.antoniovirgaarchitecte.com
10–11	Jean-Marc Palisse, stylist Caroline Clavier, architect Étienne Herpin, designer Chiara Monteleone-Travia
12 left	Pierrick Verny, stylist Laurence Botta-Delannoy, architect Mark Mertens, www.amdesigns.com
12 centre	Nicolas Millet, stylist Julie Daurel, architect Joseph Hiriart
12 right	Jean-Marc Palisse, stylist Agnès Benoit, www.roomshotel.ge
13	Christophe Dugied, stylist Caroline Mesnil, designer Véronique Piedeleu, www.caravane.fr
14	Jo Pesendorfer, stylist Aurélie des Robert
15 left	Jean-Marc Palisse, stylist Alix de Dives, designer Arnaud Caffort
15 right	Nicolas Mathéus, stylist Laurence Dougier, architect Antonio Virga, www.antoniovirgaarchitecte.com
16	Frédéric Vasseur, stylist Laurence Dougier, designer Catherine Schmit
17 top left	Jean-Marc Palisse, stylist Alix de Dives, designer Mark Homewood, www.designersguild.com
17 top right	Jo Pesendorfer, stylist Aurélie des Robert
17 below right	Eric d'Hérouville, stylist Marie-Maud Levron, architect Christophe Bachmann, www.lamaisonpavie.com
18–21	Jean-Marc Palisse, stylist Alix de Dives, designer Arnaud Caffort
22–25	Jean-Marc Palisse, stylist Caroline Clavier, architect Étienne Herpin, designer Chiara Monteleone-Travia
26-31	Frédéric Vasseur, stylist Laurence Dougier, designer Manfred Geserick
32	Pia van Spaendonck, stylist Marie-Maud Levron www.villa-augustus.nl
33	François du Chatenet, stylist Pascale de la Cochetière, designer Anouk Dossin
34	Albert Font, stylist Françoise Lefébure, architect, Amelia Molina, designer Anne Dimmers
35	François du Chatenet, stylist Pascale de la Cochetière, designer Anouk Dossin
36-39	Jean-Marc Palisse, stylist Alix de Dives, architect Marion Méchet
40–43	Patrick van Robaeys, stylist Stéphanie Boiteux-Gallard
44–45	Patrice Gavand, stylist Julie Daurel, designer Karine Laurent
46	Jean-Marc Palisse, stylist Amandine Schira, architect Christophe Ducharme, www.c-ducharme-architecte.com
47 top	Nicolas Mathéus, stylist Laurence Dougier, designer Emma Wilson
47 below	Pierrick Verny, stylist Laurence Botta-Delannoy, designer Mark Mertens, www.amdesigns.com
48-53	Bénédicte Ausset-Drummond, stylist Catherine Cornille
54-57	Pierrick Verny, stylist Muriel Gauthier, www.maison-collongue.com
58-61	Henri del Olmo, stylist Caroline Guiol, architect Karine Striga
62-67	Nicolas Mathéus, stylist Laurence Dougier, designers Michel Peraches and Eric Miele
68	François Goudier, stylist Marie Audhuy
69	Jean-Marc Palisse, stylist Amandine Schira, architect Christophe Ducharme, www.c-ducharme-architecte.com
70	Christophe Dugied, stylist Caroline Mesnil, designer Véronique Piedeleu, www.caravane.fr
71 top left and right	Jean-Marc Palisse, stylist Caroline Clavier, architect Lacvivier & Limal, designer Florence Lopez
71 below	Christophe Dugied, stylist Barbara Divry, designer Jean-Yves Pannetier
72–75	Henri del Olmo, stylist Caroline Guiol, architects Henry Roussel and Eric Steiner www.adrsarl.com
76-79	Stephen Clément, stylist Amandine Schira, architect Pierre Marmouget
80-85	Bernard Touillon, stylist Laurence Botta-Delannoy, designer Gérard Faivre
86-89	Nicolas Millet, stylist Noémi Barré, designer Frank Schmidt
90 left	Guillaume de Laubier, designer Jacques Grange
90-91	Jean-Marc Palisse, stylist Léa Delpont
92	Nicolas Mathéus, stylist Laurence Dougier, designer Emma Wilson
93	Henri del Olmo, stylist Françoise Lefébure, designer Philippe Xerri
94–97	Nicolas Matheus, stylist Laurence Dougier, designer Irène Silvagni
98–101	Eric d'Hérouville, stylist Marie-Maud Levron, www.lovelanecaravans.com
102–107	Jean-Marc Palisse, stylist Caroline Clavier, www.lestroisgarcons.com
108–113	Jean-Marc Palisse, stylist Alix de Dives, designer Sacha Walckoff
114–115	Nicolas Mathéus, stylist Laurence Dougier, architect Christophe Ducharme, www.c-ducharme-architecte.com
116	Henri del Olmo, stylist Caroline Guiol, architects Henry Roussel and Eric Steiner www.adrsarl.com
117	Jean-Marc Palisse, stylist Alix de Dives, architect Marion Méchet
118	Christophe Dugied, stylist Caroline Mesnil, designer Véronique Piedeleu, www.caravane.fr
119 left	Christophe Dugied, stylist Caroline Mesnil, designer Véronique Piedeleu, www.caravane.fr
119 right	François du Chatenet, stylist Pascale de la Cochetière, architects and designers Anouchka and Laurent Colin, www.handcraftanddesign.com
120 top left	Jean-Marc Palisse, stylist Caroline Clavier, architects Brenda Altmayer and Sabine Van Vlaenderen
120 below left	Jean-Marc Palisse, stylist Caroline Clavier, architect Lacvivier & Limal, designer Florence Lopez
120 below right	Nicolas Mathéus, stylist Laurence Dougier, designer Irène Silvagni
121	Jean-Marc Palisse, stylist Aurélie des Robert, designers Stéphane Verdino and Frédérick Foubet-Marzorati
122 left and centre	François Goudier, stylist Marie Audhuy
123 right	Christophe Dugied, stylist Barbara Divry, designer Jean-Yves Pannetier
124 left	Guillaume de Laubier, designer Jacques Grange
124 right	Jean-Marc Palisse, stylist Léa Delpont
125 left	Patrick Van Robaeys, stylist Stéphanie Boiteux-Gallard
125 centre	Nicolas Millet, stylist Noémie Barré, designer Frank Schmidt
125 right	Jean-Marc Palisse, stylist Alix de Dives, architect Christophe Ducharme, www.c-ducharme-architecte.com, designer Jean-Michel Wilmotte
126 top left	Frédéric Guigue and Bruno Suet, stylist Caroline Guiol, artist Gérard Drouillet
126 top right	Nicolas Mathéus, stylist Laurence Dougier, architect Antonio Virga, www.antoniovirgaarchitecte.com
126 below left	Nicolas Millet, stylist Amandine Schira, architect Pierre Marmouget
126 below right	Bruno Suet, stylist Francoise Lefébure
127 top left	Bruno Suet, stylist Francoise Lefébure
127 top right	Eric d'Hérouville, stylist Marie-Maud Levron, designer Aurélie Lécuyer
127 below left	François du Chatenet, stylist Pascale de la Cochetière, designer Anouk Dossin
127 below right	Pierrick Verny, stylist Muriel Gauthier, www.maison-collongue.com
128	Pierrick Verny, stylist Laurence Botta-Delannoy, architect Mark Mertens, www.amdesigns.com
129 top left	Stephen Clément, stylist Amandine Schira, architect Pierre Marmouget
129 top right	Frédéric Vasseur, stylist Laurence Dougier, designer Catherine Schmit
129 below left	Jean-Marc Palisse, stylist Caroline Clavier, architects Brenda Altmayer and Sabine Van Vlaenderen
129 below right	François du Chatenet, stylist Pascale de la Cochetière, designer Anouk Dossin
130 top left	François du Chatenet, stylist Pascale de la Cochetière, designers Anouchka and Laurent Colin, www.handcraftanddesign.com
130 below left	Eric d'Hérouville, stylist Marie-Maud Levron, designer Valérie Foster
130 below centre	Albert Font, stylist Françoise Lefébure, architect Amelia Molina
130 below right	Jean-Marc Palisse, stylist Caroline Clavier, architects Brenda Altmayer and Sabine Van Vlaenderen
131	Jean-Marc Palisse, stylist Caroline Clavier, architect Étienne Herpin, designer Chiara Monteleone-Travia
132 top left	Jean-Marc Palisse, stylist Alix de Dives, architect Christophe Ducharme www.c-ducharme-architecte.com designer Jean-Michel Wilmotte
132 below left	Bernard Touillon, stylist Laurence Botta-Delannoy, designer Gérard Faivre
132 right	Nicolas Mathéus, stylist Laurence Dougier, architect Antonio Virga,
133 left	Nicolas Mathéus, stylist Laurence Dougier,
133 right	Frédéric Guigue and Bruno Suet, stylist Caroline Guiol, artist Gérard Drouillet
134 top left	Henri del Olmo, stylist Caroline Guiol, architect Karine Striga
134 top right	Frédéric Guigue and Bruno Suet, stylist Caroline Guiol, artist Gérard Drouillet
134 below left	Jean-Marc Palisse, stylist Caroline Clavier, architects Lacvivier & Limal, designer Florence Lopez www.florencelopez.com
135 top right	Jean-Marc Palisse, stylist Alix de Dives, designer Arnaud Caffort
135 below	Guillaume de Laubier, designer Jacques Grange
136 top right	François du Chatenet, stylist Pascale de la Cochetière, designer Laure Vial du Chatenet, www.maisoncaumont.com
136 below left	Pia van Spaendonck, stylist Marie-Maud Levron, www.un-jour-en-auvergne.com
136 below right	Nicolas Mathéus, stylist Laurence Dougier, designer Irène Silvagni
137 top right	Nicolas Mathéus, stylist Laurence Dougier, designer Irène Silvagni
137 below left	Nicolas Mathéus, stylist Laurence Dougier, architect Antonio Virga www.antoniovirgaarchitecte.com
137 below right	Nicolas Mathéus, stylist Laurence Dougier, designers Michel Peraches and Eric Miele
138 top left	Stephen Clément, stylist Amandine Schira, architect Pierre Marmouget
138 below left	Nicolas Millet, stylist Noémie Barré, designer Frank Schmidt

138 below centre Jean-Marc Palisse, stylist Caroline Clavier, architect Étienne Herpin, designer Chiara Monteleone-Travia
138 below right François du Chatenet, stylist Pascale de la Cochetière, designer Laure Vial du Chatenet, www.maisoncaumont.com
139 Frédéric Guigue and Bruno Suet, stylist Caroline Guiol, artist Gérard Drouillet
140 left Henri del Olmo, stylist Caroline Guiol, architects Henry Roussel and Eric Steiner www.adrsarl.com
140 right Nicolas Mathéus, stylist Laurence Dougier, designer Emma Wilson
141 Jean-Marc Palisse, stylist Léa Delpont
142 Jean-Marc Palisse, stylist Caroline Clavier, architects Lacvivier & Limal, designer Florence Lopez www.florencelopez.com
143 left Henri del Olmo, stylist Caroline Guiol, architect Karine Striga
143 right François Goudier, stylist Marie Audhuy
144 Jean-Marc Palisse, stylist Alix de Dives, designer Mark Homewood www.designersguild.com
145 Henri del Olmo, stylist Caroline Guiol, architect Karine Striga
146 top right Nicolas Mathéus, stylist Emmanuelle Ponsan, www.sources-caudalie.com
146 below left Jean-Marc Palisse, stylist Agnès Benoit, www.roomshotel.ge
146 below right Pierrick Verny, stylist Muriel Gauthier, www.maison-collongue.com
146/7 Albert Font, stylist Françoise Lefébure, architect Amelia Molina
147 left Nicolas Millet, stylist Julie Daurel
147 right Jean-Marc Palisse, stylist Alix de Dives, architect Christophe Ducharme www.c-ducharme-architecte.com, designer Jean-Michel Wilmotte
148 Frédéric Vasseur, stylist Laurence Dougier, designer Manfred Geserick
148/9 Jean-Marc Palisse, stylist Aurélie des Robert, designers Stéphane Verdino, Frédérick Foubet-Marzorati
149 Frédéric Guigue, Bruno Suet, stylist Caroline Guiol, artist Gérard Drouillet
150 left François du Chatenet, stylist Pascale de la Cochetière, designer Anouk Dossin
150 right Christophe Dugied, stylist Barbara Divry, designer Jean-Yves Pannetier
151 Christophe Dugied, stylist Virginie Duboscq
152 Bruno Suet, stylist Françoise Lefébure
153 Jean-Marc Palisse, stylist Caroline Clavier, designer Bambi Sloan
154 left Nicolas Mathéus, stylist Laurence Dougier, designer Emma Wilson
154 right Nicolas Mathéus, stylist Laurence Dougier, designer Emma Wilson
155 left Jean-Marc Palisse, stylist Caroline Clavier, architects Brenda Altmayer, Sabine Van Vlaenderen
155 right Pierrick Verny, stylist Muriel Gauthier, www.maison-collongue.com
156 Nicolas Mathéus, stylist Laurence Dougier
157 Nicolas Mathéus, stylist Laurence Dougier
158 left Jo Pesendorfer, stylist Aurélie des Robert
158 right Nicolas Millet, stylist Julie Daurel
159 left Nicolas Millet, stylist Julie Daurel
159 right Henri del Olmo, stylist Caroline Guiol, Henry Roussel, Éric Steiner, www.adrsarl.com
160 top left François du Chatenet, stylist Pascale de la Cochetière, designer Anouk Dossin
160 below left François du Chatenet, stylist Pascale de la Cochetière, designer Anouk Dossin
160 right Guillaume de Laubier, designer Jacques Grange
161 François du Chatenet, stylist Pascale de la Cochetière, designer Anouk Dossin
162 top left Stephen Clément, stylist Amandine Schira, architect Pierre Marmouget
162 below left Stephen Clément, stylist Amandine Schira, architect Pierre Marmouget
162 top right Nicolas Millet, stylist Noémie Barré, designer Frank Schmidt
163 Nicolas Millet, stylist Noémie Barré, designer Frank Schmidt
164 top left Nicolas Millet, stylist Julie Daurel
164 top right Nicolas Millet, stylist Julie Daurel
164 below left Jean-Marc Palisse, stylist Alix de Dives, designer Mark Homewood www.designersguild.com
164 below right Jean-Marc Palisse, stylist Caroline Clavier, designer Bambi Sloan
165 top left Bernard Touillon, stylist Laurence Botta-Delannoy, designer Gérard Faivre
165 right Bernard Touillon, stylist Laurence Botta-Delannoy, designer Gérard Faivre
166 left Henri del Olmo, stylist Caroline Guiol, architects Henry Roussel, Éric Steiner, www.adrsarl.com
166 right Christophe Dugied, stylist Barbara Divry, designer Jean-Yves Pannetier
167 Nicolas Millet, stylist Noémie Barré, designer Frank Schmidt
168 left Henri del Olmo, stylist Caroline Guiol, architects Henry Roussel, Éric Steiner, www.adrsarl.com
168 top right Christophe Dugied, stylist Caroline Mesnil, designer Véronique Piedeleu, www.caravane.fr
168 below right Patrick van Robaeys, stylist Stéphanie Boiteux-Gallard
169 left Jean-Marc Palisse, stylist Caroline Clavier, designer Bambi Sloan
169 right Jean-Marc Palisse, stylist Caroline Clavier, designer Bambi Sloan
170 top left Frédéric Vasseur, stylist Laurence Dougier, designer Catherine Schmit, artist Raymond Hains, Galerie W
170 top right Jean-Marc Palisse, stylist Aurélie des Robert, designers Stéphane Verdino, Frédérick Foubet-Marzorati
170 below left Jean-Marc Palisse, stylist Alix de Dives, architect Marion Méchet, artist Romano Zanotti
171 Frédéric Vasseur, stylist Laurence Dougier, designer Catherine Schmit, artist Pierre Dimitrienko
172 left Jean-Marc Palisse, stylist Alix de Dives, designer Mark Homewood www.designersguild.com

172 right Jean-Marc Palisse, stylist Alix de Dives, designer Mark Homewood www.designersguild.com
173 top left Henri del Olmo, stylist Caroline Guiol, architects Henry Roussel, Éric Steiner, www.adrsarl.com
173 top right Frédéric Guigue, Bruno Suet, stylist Caroline Guiol, artist Gérard Drouillet
173 below right Jean-Marc Palisse, stylist Alix de Dives, designer Arnaud Caffort
174/175 François du Chatenet, stylist Pascale de la Cochetière, designer Laure Vial du Chatenet www.maisoncaumont.com
176 left Nicolas Mathéus, stylist Emmanuelle Ponsan, www.sources-caudalie.com
176 centre Éric d'Hérouville, stylist Marie-Maud Levron, designer Valérie Foster
176 right Nicolas Mathéus, stylist Emmanuelle Ponsan, www.sources-caudalie.com
177 Jean-Marc Palisse, stylist Alix de Dives, architect Christophe Ducharme www.c-ducharme-architecte.com, designer Jean-Michel Wilmotte
178/179 Nicolas Mathéus, stylist Laurence Dougier, architect Antonio Virga, www.antoniovirgaarchitecte.com
180 Nicolas Mathéus, stylist Laurence Dougier, architect Christophe Ducharme www.c-ducharme-architecte.com
181 Nicolas Mathéus, stylist Emmanuelle Ponsan, www.sources-caudalie.com
182/183 Bruno Suet, stylist Françoise Lefébure
184/185 François du Chatenet, stylist Pascale de la Cochetière, designers Anouchka and Laurent Colin, www.handcraftanddesign.com
186 Jean-Marc Palisse, stylist Alix de Dives, designer Mark Homewood www.designersguild.com
187 Frédéric Vasseur, Laurence Dougier, designer Catherine Schmit
188/189 Jo Pesendorfer, stylist Aurélie des Robert
190 top Nicolas Mathéus, stylist Laurence Dougier, designer Emma Wilson
190 below Nicolas Mathéus, stylist Laurence Dougier
191 Henri del Olmo, stylist Françoise Lefébure, designer Philippe Xerri
192/193 Pierrick Verny, stylist Laurence Botta-Delannoy, designer Mark Mertens, www.amdesigns.com
194 Nicolas Mathéus, stylist Laurence Dougier
195 top Pia von Spaendonck, stylist Marie-Maud Levron, www.villa-augustus.nl
195 below Nicolas Mathéus, stylist Laurence Dougier
196/197 Nicolas Mathéus, stylist Laurence Dougier, architect Antonio Virga, www.antoniovirgaarchitecte.com
198 Jean-Marc Palisse, stylist Alix de Dives, designer Mark Homewood www.designersguild.com
199 left Bruno Suet, stylist Françoise Lefébure
199 right Christophe Dugied, stylist Barbara Divry, designer Jean-Yves Pannetier
200 Corinne Schanté-Angelé, stylist Marie Lacire, designer Anna Boutigny, www.portobello-paris.com
201 Christophe Dugied, stylist Virginie Duboscq
202 left Jo Pesendorfer, stylist Aurélie des Robert
202 right Bernard Touillon, stylist Laurence Botta-Delannoy, designer Gérard Faivre
203 Stephen Clément, stylist Amandine Schira, architect Pierre Marmouget
204 top left Pia van Spaendonck, stylist Marie-Maud Levron, www.villa-augustus.nl
204 top right Nicolas Mathéus, stylist Laurence Dougier, designer Emma Wilson
204 below left Nicolas Mathéus, stylist Laurence Dougier, designer Irène Silvagni
204 below right Bernard Touillon, stylist Laurence Botta-Delannoy, designer Gérard Faivre
205 top right Henri del Olmo, stylist Caroline Guiol, architect Karine Striga
205 below left Nicolas Mathéus, stylist Laurence Dougier, designer Irène Silvagni
205 below right Nicolas Mathéus, stylist Laurence Dougier, designer Irène Silvagni
206 Corinne Schanté-Angelé, stylist Marie Lacire, designer Anna Boutigny, www.portobello-paris.com
207 Christophe Dugied, stylist Barbara Divry, designer Jean-Yves Pannetier
208 top/below Patrice Gavand, stylist Julie Daurel, designer Karine Laurent
208/209 Éric d'Hérouville, stylist Marie-Maud Levron, architect Christophe Bachmann, www.lamaisonpavie.com
210 Henri del Olmo, stylist Françoise Lefébure, designer Philippe Xerri
211 Jean-Marc Palisse, stylist Caroline Clavier, designer Bambi Sloan
212 Jean-Marc Palisse, stylist Alix de Dives, designer Mark Homewood www.designersguild.com
213 Stephen Clément, stylist Amandine Schira, architect Pierre Marmouget
214 left Patrice Gavand, stylist Julie Daurel, designer Karine Laurent
214 right Jean-Marc Palisse, stylist Caroline Clavier, www.lestroisgarcons.com
215 Nicolas Mathéus, stylist Laurence Dougier, designers Michel Peraches, Eric Miele
216 Éric d'Hérouville, stylist Marie-Maud Levron, designer Pascale Nivet
217 Henri del Olmo, stylist Caroline Guiol, architects Henry Roussel, Éric Steiner, www.adrsarl.com
218 left Pia van Spaendonck, stylist Marie-Maud Levron, www.villa-augustus.nl
218 right François du Chatenet, stylist Pascale de la Cochetière, designers Anouchka and Laurent Colin, www.handcraftanddesign.com
219 François du Chatenet, stylist Pascale de la Cochetière, designers Anouchka and Laurent Colin, www.handcraftanddesign.com
220 top left François du Chatenet, stylist Pascale de la Cochetière, designer Laure Vial du Chatenet www.maisoncaumont.com
220 below right Nicolas Millet, stylist Julie Daurel
221 Nicolas Millet, stylist Julie Daurel
224 Bénédicte Ausset-Drummond, stylist Catherine Cornille